BTEC First

2nd edition
BUSINESS
Assessment & Delivery Resource

Catherine Richards

Carol Carysforth

Mike Neild

www.heinemann.co.uk
- ✓ Free online support
- ✓ Useful weblinks
- ✓ 24 hour online ordering

01865 888058

Heinemann Educational Publishers
Halley Court, Jordan Hill, Oxford OX2 8EJ
Part of Harcourt Education

Heinemann is the registered trademark of
Harcourt Education Limited

Text © 2006 Harcourt, Carol Carysforth and Mike Neild

First published 2006

10 09 08 07 06

10 9 8 7 6 5 4 3 2 1

British Library Cataloguing in Publication Data is available
from the British Library on request.

10-digit ISBN: 0 435499 08 4
13-digit ISBN: 978 0 435499 08 2

Copyright notice
All rights reserved. No part of this publication may be reproduced in any form or by any means (including photocopying or storing it in any medium by electronic means and whether or not transiently or incidentally to some other use of this publication) without the written permission of the copyright owner, except in accordance with the provisions of the Copyright, Designs and Patents Act 1988 or under the terms of a licence issued by the Copyright Licensing Agency, 90 Tottenham Court Road, London W1T 4LP. Applications for the copyright owner's written permission should be addressed to the publisher.

Edited by designed by and typeset by Bookcraft Ltd, Stroud, Gloucestershire
Original illustrations © Harcourt Education Limited, 2006
Illustrated by Alex Lowe and Danny McKenzie

Cover design by Peter Stratton
Cover photo: © Corbis
Printed by Athenaeum Press Ltd

Acknowledgements
The authors and publishers are grateful to those who have given permission to reproduce material. Every effort has been made to contact copyright holders of material reproduced in this book. Any omissions will be rectified in subsequent printings if notice is given to the publishers.

Photographs, web page images and software displays
Book: Aquabella Group plc, p. 13; easyJet airline company limited (from easyJet website), p. 15; © Dorset Police 2006, p. 23; The Dorchester London, p. 42; Palm Court Hotel, Malta/Malta Bargains Ltd, p. 44; Bacardi Martini Ltd, p. 115; DSG Retail Ltd, p. 160; Rubberball Productions, p. 169; British Airways, p. 181; Stoats Porridge Bars, p. 202

CD-ROM file: Deere and Company (farm), p. 4; Corbis (factory), p. 4; PhotoDisc/Brofsky Studio Inc. (bank), p. 4; WebEx Communications Inc., p. 95; PhotoDisc/John A. Rizzo, p. 129

PowerPoint slides: Harcourt Education Ltd/Jules Selmes, Unit 4, slide 2; Bananastock, Unit 4, slides 3 and 5 (boy); AAF/Harcourt Education Ltd/Tudor Photography, Unit 4, slide 5 (girl)

Tel: 01865 888058 www.heinemann.co.uk

Contents

Introduction	**1**
Unit 1 Exploring business purposes	**3**
Activities	10
Exemplar assignment	26
Resources	30
Unit 2 Developing customer relations	**31**
Activities	37
Exemplar assignment	50
Resources	57
Unit 3 Investigating financial control	**58**
Activities	62
Exemplar assignment	71
Resources	75
Unit 4 Business communication	**76**
Activities	81
Exemplar assignment	95
Resources	102
Unit 5 People in organisations	**103**
Activities	109
Exemplar assignment	121
Resources	133
Unit 6 Providing business and administration support	**134**
Activities	138
Exemplar assignment	150
Resources	154
Unit 7 Personal selling	**155**
Activities	159
Exemplar assignment	172
Resources	176
Unit 8 Doing business online	**177**
Activities	181
Exemplar assignment	193
Resources	196
Unit 9 Exploring business enterprise	**197**
Activities	202
Exemplar assignment	212
Resources	218

Introduction

This file is designed to support the BTEC First Diploma and BTEC First Certificate Business Courses by providing additional support material that can be used in conjunction with the BTEC First Business student book.

The resource file is packed with additional activities including case studies, discussions, information research, presentations and worksheets that are presented in an easy-to-use format and can be given out as group or individual exercises.

The resource file covers the following compulsory units:

- Exploring business purposes*†
- Developing customer relations*
- Investigating financial control*

 * Compulsory units for BTEC First Diploma
 † Compulsory unit for BTEC First Certificate

Centres may then pick from the following specialist units:

- Business communication
- People in organisations
- Providing business and administration support
- Personal selling
- Doing business online
- Exploring business enterprise

Two specialist units are required for the BTEC First Certificate, and three specialist units are required for the BTEC First Diploma.

Within the qualifications there is an option to do Unit 10 Starting a Small Business, which is available at Level 3. Unit 10 is not included within this resource file.

Each unit contains an overview with relevant data about the unit, including the learning outcomes of the unit and the Pass, Merit and Distinction criteria that are covered by the unit..

An At-a-glance activity grid is provided to make selection of the tasks very easy. The tasks are referenced by learning outcome and by the individual performance criteria that the activity aims to work towards. Page references to the *BTEC First Business* student book are also included to locate information that can be used to support the activities.

A range of different activities is provided within each of the units. The At-a-glance grid includes delivery notes with an explanation of what each activity is about, and lists any additional resources that may be required for the activity.

Each unit also contains an Exemplar Assignment and a list of resources – publications and websites – that may help to support the unit.

We are sure that this resource file and accompanying CD-ROM will provide an invaluable resource for the delivery of the BTEC First Diploma and BTEC First Certificate Business courses. We wish you and your students every success on these courses.

Introduction

The CD-ROM

On the accompanying CD-ROM, a PowerPoint presentation has been included for each unit, with supporting guidance notes. Relevant material can be presented to students in a matter of minutes, as well as copies of the material that can be customised to your needs. This helps to enhance the use of ILT within lessons to support individual units.

All the worksheet activities of the resource file are also on the CD-ROM, together with all the pages from the printed part of this Assessment and Delivery Resource. Tutors can adjust the activities to reflect local situations or the specific needs of particular groups of students.

Answers to the Activities and Over to You questions, as well as the Case Study – Assessment Practice sections in the *BTEC First Business* student book are also included on the CD-ROM to support delivery of these features.

Accessing the CD-ROM

Insert the CD into your computer's CD-ROM drive and it should run automatically.

If your PC does not support autorun:

Go to **My Computer** and double-click on the CD-ROM drive. The CD-ROM should now run. If it still does not run, but instead displays a list of the files on the CD-ROM:

Double-click on the **Files** folder and then double-click on the **BTEC-First-Business.pdf** file.

Details on how to access the files on the CD-ROM can be found in the section called **How to use this CD-ROM** on the CD itself.

Websites

Please note that the examples of websites suggested in this Assessment and Delivery Resource were up to date at the time of writing. It is essential for tutors to preview each site before using it, to ensure that the URL is still accurate and the content is appropriate. We suggest that tutors bookmark useful sites and consider enabling students to access them through the school or college Intranet.

Unit 1 Exploring business purposes

Unit overview

Unit 1 is a core unit for both the BTEC First Certificate and BTEC First Diploma qualifications in Business. The unit is designed to give learners a clear background and description of why different businesses exist, by building on the knowledge that they have gained of the world around them.

This unit seeks to help learners gain an appreciation of how complicated the business world is, and that businesses are adapting and changing because of the different influences around them on a local, national, European and international scale.

As part of this unit, learners will be shown how businesses are classified according to their different types of ownership and industrial sector, while also taking into account those aims and objectives that drive the future planning and operations of the organisations.

Learners will have the opportunity to study the different functional areas that carry out the day-to-day operations, which should enable them to gain greater understanding of the business in preparation for work experience or seeking employment.

Suggested activities

The table on the following pages shows how activities in this Assessment and Delivery Resource cover the four different outcomes of the Unit. There is a variety of tasks, including discussion material, worksheets, case studies and presentation material.

The research tasks have been prepared to allow students to gather evidence in note form to help them produce their own work.

How this unit will be assessed

To gain a Pass, learners will need to:

P1 describe four different types of business organisations in terms of purpose, ownership, size and scale

P2 describe the primary, secondary and tertiary classifications of business activities using local and national examples

P3 describe the purpose of setting aims and objectives for businesses

P4 describe the functional areas and their main purposes within business organisations.

To gain a Merit requires learners to complete all the Pass requirements plus the Merit requirements, where they need to:

M1 compare and contrast the ownership, aims and objectives of two selected businesses

M2 explain areas of growth or decline in the primary, secondary and tertiary classifications of business activities

M3 explain the interaction of functional areas and how they relate to each other in two selected businesses.

To gain a Distinction requires a learner to complete all the Pass and Merit requirements plus the Distinction requirement, where they need to:

D1 evaluate how the functional areas contribute to the aims and objectives of the two selected businesses.

Learning outcomes

The unit is based on the following learning outcomes:

1. Understand the nature of business and ownership
2. Understand the classification of business activities
3. Understand business aims and objectives in different sectors
4. Know the main functional areas that support business organisations.

© Harcourt Education 2006

At-a-glance

Activity type and description	Delivery notes	Extra resources	Links to grading criteria	Links to student book
Outcome 1 Understand the nature of business and ownership Aims to give students an idea about the different purposes of business and the way that ownership impacts on those businesses				
1.1 Introductory worksheet: What's their purpose?	Intended to help students consider what a business does and why it exists, e.g. for profit or not for profit. This activity can also be used to encourage learners to think about the different numbers of businesses that are in operation for different purposes and the difference between the public and private sectors.	Worksheet on CD-ROM, Internet access, company brochures	P1	Pages 2–3
1.2 Worksheet: Different types of ownership	Helps students build on their understanding of material available in the textbook.	Worksheet on CD-ROM	P1, M1	Pages 3–6
1.3 Worksheet: Dear Jane	Letter from a sole trader asking for advice from the students about whether or not to change the business ownership from sole trader to limited company. Students will need to use the student book to help them.	Worksheet on CD-ROM	P1	Page 4
1.4 Discussion: Shareholders' mind-map	Asks students to consider the problems or benefits an individual business may have when dealing with its shareholders as a PLC, rather than as a private limited company – possible answers could include loss of control, additional pressure from shareholders who want dividends in the short term rather than investment in the longer term, and so on.	Large pieces of paper or flipchart, pens	M1	Pages 3–4
1.5 Research activity: Size and scale research	Provided for students who wish to choose their own businesses to study for P1 and M1, to add notes on the purpose, ownership, size and scale of the business. Students are encouraged to make notes within the boxes that can be written up later as part of their assessed work.	Internet access, company literature	P1, M1	Pages 7–11

Activity type and description	Delivery notes	Extra resources	Links to grading criteria	Links to student book
1.6 Plenary activity: True or false?	Quick quiz for students to confirm their understanding of key concepts.		P1	Pages 2–11
Outcome 2 Understand the classification of business activities Teaches students how to classify business activities according to the primary, secondary and tertiary sectors				
1.7 Introductory activity: Sector?	This activity can be used in two ways: to stimulate the concept and idea of primary, secondary and tertiary or to assess prior knowledge as students may be aware of these notions from their studies of geography. This activity allows the teacher to judge the level of existing knowledge.	Extra paper, pens	P2	Page 12
1.8 Worksheet: PST?	This activity provides three pictures representing primary (a farm), secondary (a factory production line) and tertiary (a bank). Students are asked to write the businesses listed (and any other businesses that you wish to include on the board as well), into the spaces provided.	Board/pen, worksheet on CD-ROM	P2	Pages 12–16
1.9 Case study: New Forest Barramundi	Designed to get students thinking about the growth and decline of specific types of businesses within the context of the sector as a whole. It is to be used to remind students that, whilst fishing in general is in decline, there are still examples where new niches are able to expand.	Internet or newpaper articles on fishing industry and food trends	P2, M2	Pages 17–20
1.10 Discussion activity: Growth or decline in the industrial sectors?	This activity gives students the chance to look at information on the growth or decline of the sectors as a graph. This can be used to support their evidence for M2.	Newspaper or Internet articles about sector growth/ decline	M2	Pages 17–20
1.11 Research activity: Searching sectors	Supports the completion of the assignment by allowing students to make notes and look up businesses that are in their own locality that are expanding or declining. This task usefully supports M2.	Internet access	M2	Pages 17–20

BTEC First Business

Activity type and description	Delivery notes	Extra resources	Links to grading criteria	Links to student book
1.12 Case study: Cadbury	Stimulates students into thinking how costs affect the manufacturing process and the way that large organisations can benefit from moving operations elsewhere. This also helps to support thinking about the decline of different sectors in the UK.		P2, M2	Pages 17–20
1.13 Plenary activity (gapped table): Declining or growing?	Seeks to remind and revise industrial sectors by using real examples and asking students to fill in the gaps	Internet access, business sections of newspapers	P2	Pages 17–20
Outcome 3 Understand business aims and objectives in different sectors Helps students to learn about the way that aims and objectives are similar or different between sectors. The activities are designed to give students the opportunity to work with some objectives and to consider the way that objectives are used to plan the future of a business.				
1.14 Introductory activity: Guess the aim	Provides students with the opportunity to match some aims to different businesses as a starter activity. This activity allows them to consider the wording that businesses use when writing their objectives, e.g. not usually mentioning profit. This task could be further extended by asking students to write possible objectives to support those aims or to produce their own researched version of the game that they can try out on their peer group.		P1, P3, M1	Pages 21–22
1.15 Worksheet: Short-term or long-term	Gives students an opportunity to consider that some objectives will take longer than others and the type of objectives that can be completed in a shorter amount of time rather than those that need to be done over a number of years.	Worksheet on CD-ROM	P3	Pages 21–22
1.16 Worksheet: Getting smarter	Introduces students to the concept of SMART and the way that suitable objectives can make the job of planning and monitoring much easier than those which are not SMART.	Worksheet on CD-ROM	P3	Page 22

Exploring business purposes

Activity type and description	Delivery notes	Extra resources	Links to grading criteria	Links to student book
1.17 Discussion activity: easyJet	Allows students to think about successful enterprises that have overall guiding aims throughout their group of companies. easyJet has the overriding concept of low cost, low price. Students are encouraged to think how successful this aim is for all of the different parts of the EasyGroup. This could be extended for students by considering what competitors are doing.	Internet access to easy.com	P3, M1	Pages 23–26
1.18 Research activity: Vision and mission statements	Designed to help students gather evidence on the different types of aims businesses have, including whether or not they write a vision or mission statement. They examine four different examples, so two of these may be considered in more detail as part of the M1 work.	Internet access or company literature	P1, M1	Pages 23–26
1.19 Plenary activity: Being the Principal!	To consolidate learning, students are encouraged to write a set of aims and objectives for their school or college. They may find it useful to do this and then to compare their set with others in the group to find out any similarities or differences.		P1	Pages 21–26
Outcome 4 Know the main functional areas that support business organisations				
1.20 Introductory activity: What does a business do?	Gives a good opportunity for assessment or prior learning. Students are likely to have had some experience of a workplace through either work experience while at school or a part-time job. Students can group the activities with or without teacher support.	Computer or paper	P4	Page 27
1.21 Worksheet: Functional areas	Further reinforces what goes on in individual functional areas by asking students to allocate which they think are activities of the various functional areas. This should help them to consider which activities are carried out by looking at which functional areas are present in the different businesses they are studying.	Worksheet on CD-ROM	P4	Pages 27–41
1.22 Worksheet: Functional area word search	This fun activity stretches students by asking them to remember which functional areas they have learned and then to see if they can try and find them as well as describe what they mean. It can be made easier by giving the students the words.	Worksheet on CD-ROM	P4	Pages 27–41

© Harcourt Education 2006

Activity type and description	Delivery notes	Extra resources	Links to grading criteria	Links to student book
1.23 Discussion activity: Ebay	Asks students to think of the different functional areas and review them in the context of Ebay. By examining the differences in importance of the functional areas, students may also be able to consider how they interact with each other. Students working at Distinction level should be encouraged to think about how they contribute to the aims of Ebay.	Paper to make notes	P4, M3, D1	Pages 27–41
1.24 PowerPoint presentation: Different functional areas	Guides the students through the key points of each of the functional areas. This may be a useful activity to use near the beginning of the study of this outcome.	Projector	P4	Pages 27–41
1.25 Research activity: Functional area research	Allows students to start collecting notes and study the organisations they are going to use for their assessed work. Within the specification there is a recommendation that students try to get more in-depth study of fewer functional areas rather than very brief coverage of many of the functional areas, particularly to work towards achievement at the higher levels. Additional prompts are given to stretch students working towards P4, M3 and D1.	Company organisation charts	P4, M3, D1	Pages 27–42
1.26 Case study: Dorset Police Human Resources Department	Allows students to see the types of activity that a specific Human Resources Department carries out. Encourages students to assess which functional areas are most important to a particular organisation.	Internet access to Dorset Police website	P4	Pages 33–34
1.27 Discussion activity: Cooperation	Encourages students to think about the sort of information that business departments need to exchange in a real situation.	Organisation charts of company departments	P4	Pages 41–42

Exploring business purposes

Activity type and description	Delivery notes	Extra resources	Links to grading criteria	Links to student book
1.28 Plenary activity (discussion/role-play): What do we do now?	Asks students to think about how business departments must interact when solving a problem, and shows that departments can sometimes have conflicting interests. Can be run as a discussion or a role-play. For a role-play, students take on the roles of different departments, and should be given time to consider the department's position before a general discussion between departments. The teacher or a student may take the role of CEO to announce and explain the final decisions.		P4, M3, D1	Pages 41–42
1.29 Discussion activity: Who needs them?	Focusing on the less common functional areas, asks the students to think which types of businesses are likely or unlikely to have them. The lists could be extended.		P4	Pages 27–41
1.30 Plenary activity: Presentation	Giving this presentation requires students to consolidate their learning by feeding back to others in the group about what they have learned about at least two functional areas. This activity may be used as the last activity before students start their formal write-up for assessment.	Somewhere to practise verbal presentations	P4	Pages 27–42

© Harcourt Education 2006

Unit 1

1.1 Introductory worksheet: What's their purpose?

Student book pages 2–3

See CD-ROM

1.2 Worksheet: Different types of ownership

Student book pages 3–6

See CD-ROM

1.3 Worksheet: Dear Jane

Student book page 4

See CD-ROM

1.4 Discussion: Shareholders' mind-map

Student book pages 3–4

A private limited company (Ltd) needs people to invest money in the business by buying shares in the company. Public limited companies (plc) also have shareholders.

Using a mind-map, write down the benefits or problems there could be for a private limited company and compare them to those for a plc. Are there any differences in who can own shares in the two types of company?

1.5 Research: Size and scale research

Student book pages 7–11

A business can be measured in terms of its size and scale. **Size** can be measured in terms of the number of people the business employs, the value of the products or services that they sell or the number of different products/services that they produce or offer. **Scale** measures how widely that business operates – locally, nationally, on a European level or internationally.

As part of your assessed work, you will need to choose four different organisations to study and describe their purpose, ownership, size and scale (P1). Using the Internet or your textbook, complete the table below with notes to help you answer P1.

If you wish to go on to do M1, you will need to compare two of the businesses you have chosen with each other.

Name of the business	Purpose What do they actually do – their main activities?	Ownership What type of ownership do they have?	Size How many employees work for them? What is their annual turnover? How many different products/services do they sell?	Scale On what scale do they operate – local, national, European, International?

Outcome 1

1.6 Plenary activity: True or false?

Student book pages 2–11

State which of the following statements are true, and which are false.

- PLC stands for Publicity Limit Company.
- One advantage of being a sole trader is limited liability.
- Ltd stands for Public Limited Company.
- Organisations like charities need to make a profit every year.
- Anyone can buy shares within a PLC.
- Most businesses in the UK are publicly owned.
- A group of business people, such as solicitors, who run a business together often have partnership ownership.
- Cadbury is an example of a sole trader.
- Britain's largest partnership is the John Lewis Partnership.
- Public ownership means that anyone can buy shares in that organisation.

Exploring business purposes

1.7 Introductory activity: Sector?

Student book page 12

For each of the following sectors write down what you think is meant by:

- Primary sector _____
- Secondary sector _____
- Tertiary sector _____

1.8 Worksheet: PST?

Student book pages 12–16

See CD-ROM

1.9 Case study: New Forest Barramundi

Student book pages 17–20

More information at
www.aquab.com

Whilst primary industries in general have been declining in the UK, in some instances there has been an increase in production, e.g. due to the demands of people living in the UK who want to eat a fresh, low-fat fish with Omega-3 oils. New Forest Barramundi is based in Lymington, Hampshire and is now one of the largest fish farms in Europe.

Barramundi have been farmed in the UK since January 2005, and annual production increased to around 400 tonnes in 2005/6. Barramundi are traditionally produced in Australian waters, so Aquabella, the fish farm production company, have had to set up warm-water tanks in the New Forest to produce the fish. The fish were first supplied to restaurants and wholesalers, but during 2006 were also bought by the supermarket chain Waitrose.

1. Which industrial sector is New Forest Barramundi in?
2. What is the trend for the sector?
3. What is the trend for New Forest Barramundi?
4. What makes Barramundi fish so popular and what is this likely to mean for Aquabella in the future?

1.10 Discussion: Growth or decline in the industrial sectors?

Student book pages 17–20

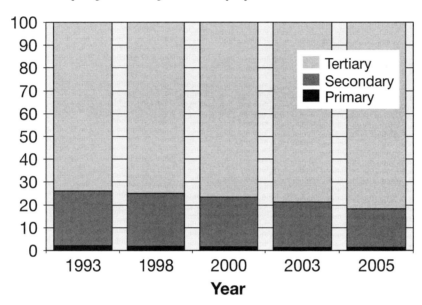

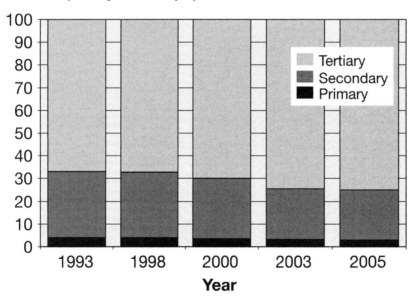

1. What do you notice is happening within the graphs in the primary, secondary and tertiary sectors?

2. Using the book and articles or information given to you by your teacher, give reasons as to why you think this is happening (P2, M2).

1.11 Research: Searching sectors

Student book pages 17–20

Using the websites www.nationalstatistics.org.uk and www.businesslink.gov.uk, search for information on the businesses/sectors that are growing or declining in your local area. Complete the table with your notes.

Businesses or sector	Growth or decline	Evidence for this

1.12 Case study: Cadbury

Student book pages 17–20

Cadbury will open a new factory in Poland by 2008 to supply the increasing demand for its brands particularly in Europe, the Middle East and Asia, which gave Cadbury a turnover of £349 million in 2004. The factory in Poland will create 300 jobs at first, and there may be the possibility to expand at a later date. Cadbury chose Poland to base its new manufacturing plants primarily because producing products is very cheap in Poland, and also the country has a good central position for distribution throughout Europe, Asia and the Middle East. This is not the first venture for Cadbury in Poland. In 1999 they acquired Wedel, a Polish chocolate brand, which trades in Poland as Cadbury Wedel.

1. Which industrial sector is Cadbury in?
2. Why did they choose to expand in to Poland?
3. How could Cadbury grow by expanding in to other industrial sectors?

1.13 Plenary activity: Declining or growing?

Student book pages 17–20

Using the Internet, fill in the gaps in the table below, so that each row describes a business and its sector.

Business sector	Example	Sector declining or growing?
Primary		Declining
	HSBC Bank	
Secondary		
	Red Cross	
		Growing
	NHS hospital	

Outcome 2

1.14 Introductory activity: Guess the aim!

Student book pages 21–22

Aims

These aims have been slightly adapted to make them easier to understand, but see if you can match the aim to the organisation.

1. To be admired all over the world for financial services and be recognised for innovation and customer focus
2. To be the number 1 leader in world travel
3. To bring inspiration and innovation to every athlete in the world
4. To ensure a quality of service from the first customer enquiry through production or processing to final delivery on time with complete customer satisfaction
5. To maintain a stable and efficient framework for money and finances
6. To organise the world's information and make it easy to understand and be useful
7. To provide our customers with safe, good value, point-to-point air services.

Businesses

	Statement number
Bank of England	
Barclays	
British Airways	
easyJet	
Google	
Nike	
Packwell D and S Ltd	

Outcome 3

1.15 Worksheet: Short-term or long-term

Student book pages 21–22

See CD-ROM

1.16 Worksheet: Getting smarter

Student book page 22

See CD-ROM

1.17 Discussion: easyJet

Student book pages 23–26

easyJet was started in 1995 by Stelios Haji-Ioannou and went from a one-route operator to being one of the largest airlines in Europe. easyJet did not offer a new service as such, because air travel already existed, but it reduced costs by not offering free meals on flights, and by flying to airports that charged lower 'airport taxes'.

The easyGroup companies have now expanded through more business planning into other budget areas.

For more information, access easyJet's website www.easyjet.com or the group at www.easy.com

1. What aim did Stelios have for his range of 'easy' services?
2. Write down the names of all the other easy companies that you have heard of.
3. For each one you have thought of, discuss whether or not you think making it low-cost, low-price is likely to work.

Exploring business purposes 19

1.18 Research activity: Vision and mission statements

Student book pages 23–26

A vision or mission statement is a way of putting the aims of an organisation into a written statement that can lead the organisation and can be viewed by anyone who is influenced or affected by the organisation (stakeholders).

Using the Internet or your textbook, examine four different published vision or mission statements.

1. What do they have in common?
2. What is different about them?
3. How do they help an organisation to plan for the future?

1.19 Plenary activity: Being the Principal!

Student book pages 21–26

Now you have learned about what is meant by aims and objectives, consider the aims that your Principal has for your college or school.

1. What do you think their vision might be?
2. Which objectives would they need to set out to help achieve that?

Outcome 3 © Harcourt Education 2006

1.20 Introductory activity: What does a business do?

Student book page 27

1. Write down as many activities as you can think of that a business does.
2. Now, taking that list of activities, can you group them at all? For example, recruiting, training and pay may all be linked to the Human Resources Department.
3. Do you know the name of the functional areas that are linked to all those activities?

1.21 Worksheet: Functional areas

Student book pages 27–41

See CD-ROM

1.22 Worksheet: Functional area word search

Student book pages 27–41

See CD-ROM

1.23 Discussion activity: Ebay

Student book pages 27–41

In small groups, discuss which of the functional areas you think would be most important for a business such as Ebay. Put them into order of importance. Now compare your results with another group – were they the same or different? Why do you think this is?

1.24 Powerpoint activity: Different functional areas

Student book pages 27–41

See CD-ROM

1.25 Research activity: Functional area research

Student book pages 27–42

For your assignment you will need to explore the main internal functional areas of your chosen business. You will need to show you understand what those functional areas do, and their purpose in the organisation. Make sure you collect information about the main functional areas in as much detail as you can. Do not collect brief information about all the departments. For Merit you will need to explain how they interact (work together) and relate to each other in two businesses. Use the table to help you make notes to write up.

Business 1

Functional area (P4)	What does it do? (P4)	How does this functional area work with other functional areas in the business? Describe the relationship with the other area in as much detail as you can

If you are going to work towards D1, you will need to give a judgement about how these functional areas contribute towards the aims and objectives of each of the two businesses.

Functional area	Give a judgment about how this functional area contributes towards the aims and objectives of Business 1 (D1)

Outcome 4

© Harcourt Education 2006

1.25 Research activity: Functional area research (continued)

Business 2

Functional area (P4)	What does it do? (P4)	How does this functional area work with other functional areas in the business? Describe the relationship with the other area in as much detail as you can

If you are going to work towards D1, you will need to give a judgement about how these functional areas contribute towards the aims and objectives of each of the two businesses.

Functional area	Give a judgment about how this functional area contributes towards the aims and objectives of Business 2 (D1)

Exploring business purposes 23

1.26 Case Study: Dorset Police Human Resources Department

Student book pages 33–34

The Human Resource Department for Dorset Police has lots of different tasks to do, which are given under eight different headings:

- **Recruitment and Selection** – they recruit and choose from the applicants who apply to work as police officers, police staff (support staff), or the special constabulary
- **Employee Relations** – this means working with trade unions and other organisations to help negotiate terms and conditions of work
- **Human Resources planning** – to plan for the future staff needs of the Dorset Police Force by working out how many new people to recruit, and additional training that might be needed for people to work towards promotion in the future
- **Education, training and development** – to offer training at the start of a person's employment and into the future
- **Organisational development and design** – to think about the best number of people needed to do various jobs, and to think about whether or not resources such as IT may be used to change and improve jobs
- **Pay benefits and other conditions of service** – to deal with issues to do with how much pay individuals receive, sick pay, pensions and so on
- **Employee services** – all other services offered: the canteen, counselling, support for employees with families, etc.
- **Communication and consultation with staff** – dealing with all aspects of working with staff by talking to them and letting them know the latest changes in the police force. They also ask people's opinions about how things can be improved, etc.

Dorset Police have lots of different job roles within HR, so you can see the variety of different work that a functional area can carry out. (Source www.dorset.police.uk)

1 Which of the tasks listed above do you think are the most important?
2 Which tasks do you think are the least important?
3 How important do you think Human Resources are to Dorset Police, and why?

Outcome 4

1.27 Discussion activity: Cooperation

Student book pages 41–42

Think of a large consumer electrical appliance manufacturer that makes several different products.

1. Which functional areas are involved in deciding which products should be made, and when, by the production department?
2. What information do the other functional areas need to give the production department?
3. What information do the other functional areas need to receive from the production department?

1.28 Plenary activity: What do we do now?

Student book pages 41–42

The Quality Manager of Whizzy Electronics plc has just discovered that, because of an incorrect machine setting in the production department, a batch of products has a defect that will cause most of them to fail within about six months of use. The products have not yet left the factory, and the fault could be fixed by fitting replacement parts, which will need to be ordered in from a supplier. The marketing department has already booked advertising slots on TV and in magazines to promote the product. The sales department has promised dates when the product will be delivered to the shops.

1. Should Whizzy Electronics just deliver the faulty products anyway?
2. If the faulty products are delivered, what is the likely result
   - in the short term?
   - in the long term?
3. Who will be involved in deciding what to do next, if the decision is made not to send the faulty products to the shops?
4. Who should be worried about the situation?
5. What should be done to avoid a repeat of the situation?

Exploring business purposes — 25

1.29 Discussion activity: Who needs them?

Student book pages 27–41

In small groups, identify

1 some types of businesses in which these functions are important enough to have major departments with their own managers:
  - safety
  - franchising or licensing
  - training.

2 some types of businesses (other than sole traders!) that would not have these functions:
  - production
  - training
  - distribution.

1.30 Plenary activity: Presentation

Student book pages 27–41

Produce a verbal presentation that lasts two minutes on two different functional areas that you have learned about within this unit or from your part-time job. Give the key points about the functional area. If you are working towards Merit or Distinction, make sure you include interactions with other areas and a judgement about how they help the business to achieve its aims and objectives.

Unit 1 Exemplar assignment

Assignment 1.4

Background to the assignment

For this assignment you will need to visit or collect evidence on Cadbury and My College.

Use information on www.cadburys.co.uk and the class handouts to help you.

This assignment is aiming to help you achieve:

P4 Describe the functional areas and their main purposes within business organisations

M3 Explain the interaction of functional areas and how they related to each other in two selected businesses.

Task 1 (P4)

Describe the functional areas and their main purposes within business organisations

You will need to consider the different areas of business that relate to Cadbury's and to My College and describe the purpose of **four** of these different areas, giving examples from both businesses. The possible functional areas include

- Human Resources
- Distribution
- Marketing
- Finance
- Sales
- Administration
- IT
- Customer Services/Student Services

For each functional area write what that area does and how it helps the business to be run giving the type of activity for each business

Task 2 (M2)

Explain the interaction of functional areas and how they relate to each other in two selected businesses

You will need to explain how your four functional areas communicate and relate to each other within each business giving as many examples as you can.

- How they communicate with each other
- How they work together

You may find it useful to compare the businesses – what do they do that is the same and what is different.

Sarah Smith

Task 1 Functional areas

I have chosen to describe the purpose of the following functional areas for Cadbury's and My College:

Human Resources

Finance

Customer/Student Services

Human Resources

Human Resources look after all the people who are employed to work at an organisation. They hire people to work for the organisation. This means they need to recruit people by advertising for new vacancies and then sort out application forms for jobs before people are chosen to come for an interview. When people have joined the business they are given a contract. This means they know how long they are going to be working there. Sometimes they are given permanent contracts and other times temporary ones. Human Resources have to plan to have enough staff to help the business. At Cadbury's they hire people to do lots of different jobs, some people work on the production line making the chocolate and some people are needed to work in other departments like IT or Marketing. Cadbury need a lot of staff as they trade all over the world and they have a tourist attraction near Birmingham called Cadbury World. My College also have to hire people but they don't need anyone to work on a production line making products like chocolate. They need teachers and people to do the paperwork. At My College if someone goes to work there the College ask them to work for six months to show that they are okay in the job before they give them a permanent contract.

Human Resources also have to check how people are working when they are employed there by checking on their progress. To do this they do appraisals once a year or sometimes more. Cadbury's and My College both do appraisals so that staff know how they are doing. These appraisals help the employees to know how they are doing and also to give them targets to improve. For a worker in Cadbury's it might be to pack more chocolate or help more visitors. For My College it might be to help students to get better results or to help them go on to higher level courses.

Human Resources are in charge of paying wages, this is known as payroll. If someone does any extra hours they are given overtime money and this needs to be paid to them. At Cadbury the employees are likely to have different pay depending on the number of hours they work so they need to make adjustments every month within HR to pay people properly. In My College overtime is not paid so if a teacher or an administrator does more hours they get time off.

If someone has a problem they also go to HR and then they can tell them their problem and hopefully HR can solve it for them. They are also in charge of paying sick pay or sorting out maternity pay if someone is having a baby. If someone is ill or is having a baby they sort out their money and pay them the right amount. They also monitor how often someone is off ill so they can help them to be off sick less if they can. In My College and Cadbury's they want to have as little time off sick so they try to think of ways to help employees to cope better with work eg giving them stress management training.

Finally Human Resources deal with training. They sort out all the different types of training that people have. They need to give training at the start of when someone works there.

Task 1

This is called induction training. They also have to sort out training for someone if they are going to do a new job or they need new skills to do their job such as needing training to work a new computer system or new ways of doing a job. At My College the teachers have induction training for the first six weeks that they work there, this is to help them know everything about the College.

Finance

The finance department is one that sorts out all the money. They have to deal with the day to day money. They pay suppliers and they take in money from sales. At Cadbury's they take payments from retailers or supermarkets who pay them for their finished chocolate. At My College the money comes from the Learning and Skills Council. They pay the money to the college for how many students they have studying there.

Cadbury's and My College both have suppliers to pay and Finance has the job of paying them. Cadbury's have to pay for raw materials so that they can make the chocolate. They also need to pay for other things like equipment such as computers, paper, ink etc.

In Cadbury's they employ lots of different people to work in the Finance Area. They have accountants who make all the accounts for the business and try to predict the money that is going to be available in the future. Cadbury's need to make a profit. At My College they only have one accountant and their job is to make sure that there is enough money to help students to pass their courses by paying for teachers and materials. Both Cadbury's and My College have to work with budgets to make sure that they don't spend too much money but My College does not need to make a profit.

Customer Services/Student Services

Customer Services and Student Services have the same job because they are trying to make sure that the customers of the business are happy. At Cadbury Customer Services deal with any complaints that there might be about any of the chocolate and arrange for people to have their money back. They also ask customers about different types of chocolate and how they can make their products even better. Student Services at My College also want to know what customers (students) think about the College and how they can make it better. At My College they do a student satisfaction survey where they find out about what students like and what they think could be improved. The College Principal looks at these to decide how they can improve things.

Assessor feedback

Sarah you have chosen three good departments to work on. Your work on Human Resources was really good and you have clearly shown their purpose for both businesses.

You have made a really good start but your work on Finance and Customer Services/Student Services needs to be improved.

For finance you need to describe more about different types of financial records and the accounts. You also should write about how each business gets money from people that owe it money – what are these people called.

For Customer/Student Services give more examples of the types of tasks that the Students Services team do at My College – giving out bus pass information, giving details about applications to University, printing timetables and so on.

You have also forgotten to include a fourth functional area so please choose one and add the information in.

If you wish to upgrade this work to Merit you will need to think about how the different functional areas work together at Cadbury's and My College.

How do Finance and HR work together – how do they communicate at both businesses?

How do HR and Customer/Student Services work and communicate together?

You need to think of different examples to explain your points.

Unit 1 Resources

Textbooks

Carysforth, C. and Neild, M., *BTEC First Business* (Heinemann, 2006)

Dransfield, R. et al., *BTEC National Business: Student Book* (Heinemann, 2004). This resource may be useful for those students operating at Distinction level who require additional information to help them.

Websites

www.bized.ac.uk	Bized business education site
www.statistics.gov.uk	Government statistics site
www.dorset.police.uk	Dorset Police website
www.ehow.com	Form of search engine with links to business information (USA-based)
www.businesslink.gov.uk	Business Link, an official government service that provides advice and information for new and small businesses
www.chamberonline.co.uk	National website for the UK chambers of commerce, providing information on current issues; allows local chambers of commerce to be located (although not all are linked to this site), as sources of information on local businesses, guest speakers, etc.
www.bsi-global.com	British Standards Institution, source of information on ISO 9000 quality management schemes

Professional bodies for practitioners in various of the specialised business functional areas include

www.ismm.co.uk	Institute of Sales and Marketing Management
www.cipd.co.uk	The Chartered Institute of Personnel and Development
www.cips.org	Chartered Institute of Purchasing and Supply

Unit 2 Developing customer relations

Unit overview

Unit 2 is a core unit for the BTEC First Diploma and a specialist unit for the BTEC First Certificate qualifications in Business. The unit aims to help students appreciate the importance of customers to each and every business whether they are offering a product or service for profit or not-for-profit.

Learners will be encouraged to think about the wider context of customers within their chosen business including developing an understanding of customer needs and expectations.

Learners will develop an appreciation and understanding of what is meant by an internal customer compared to that of an external customer.

As part of this unit learners will gain skills in understanding the need to act in a professional way and to conduct themselves appropriately in the customer service situation including appropriate communication skills. Learners will also have the chance to undertake assessments of a practical nature to demonstrate their new skills.

Monitoring and evaluation of customer feedback is also important within this unit and will allow learners to understand how improvements are made to the customer service environment based on this data.

Suggested activities

The table on the following page shows how activities in this Assessment and Delivery Resource cover the four different outcomes of the Unit. There are a variety of tasks including discussion material, worksheets, case studies and presentation material.

The research tasks have been prepared to allow students to gather evidence in note form to help them produce their own work.

How this unit will be assessed

To gain a Pass, learners will need to:

P1 describe three different types of customers and their needs and expectations

P2 demonstrate presentation and interpersonal skills in three different customer service situations

P3 describe how consistent and reliable customer service contributes to customer satisfaction

P4 describe how customer service can be monitored and evaluated.

To gain a Merit requires learners to complete all the Pass requirements plus the Merit requirements, where they need to:

M1 display a confident approach when delivering customer service to customers

M2 explain why presentation, interpersonal and communication skills are important to customer service

M3 explain how monitoring and evaluating can improve customer service for the customer, the organisation and the employee.

To gain a Distinction requires a learner to complete all the Pass and Merit requirements plus the Distinction requirements, where they need to:

D1 anticipate and meet the needs of at least three different customers in a range of situations

D2 analyse, using examples, how effective customer service benefits the customer, the organisation and the employee.

Learning outcomes

The unit is based on the following learning outcomes

1. Understand how customer service is provided in business
2. Be able to apply appropriate presentation and interpersonal skills in customer service situations
3. Know how consistent and reliable customer service contributes to customer satisfaction
4. Know how to monitor and evaluate customer service within an organisation.

© Harcourt Education 2006

At-a-glance

Activity type and description	Delivery notes	Extra resources	Links to grading criteria	Links to student book
Outcome 1 Understand how customer service is provided in business				
2.1 Introductory activity: What is customer service?	This activity is designed to get students thinking about what customer service actually means by looking at four different definitions. Students are asked to consider what is the same about the definitions, what is different and which ones they think are best or worst. Extension material is provided for students to write their own definition.	Paper, pens	P1	Pages 46–51
2.2 Worksheet: Me as the customer	This activity is designed to get students thinking about their own expectations of customer service in different scenarios. Students can then compare how their expectations are different from those of other students in their group.	Worksheet on CD-ROM	P1	Pages 46–51
2.3 Worksheet: Customer needs	This activity asks students to match the needs to the different customer groups. Four of the groups are external and two are internal, so this is an ideal opportunity to go over the internal/external concept again. For work at Distinction level, an additional question asks students to consider how they would meet the needs of three different types of customers.	Worksheet on CD-ROM	P1, D1	Pages 52–55
2.4 Worksheet: Internal or external?	Students need to work through the scenarios and indicate whether or not the scenario is an example of internal customer service or external customer service. To encourage their thinking and confirm understanding, students are also asked to write why.	Worksheet on CD-ROM	P1	Pages 52–55
2.5 Research activity: Gathering data	By completing this table in note form, students are able to collect evidence for their assessed piece of work.		P1	Pages 52–55
2.6 Plenary: Right or wrong?	As a final check on the correct or incorrect way to respond to customers – students are asked to comment on whether responses are right are wrong by explaining why or how they should be different.	Pens	P1	Pages 46–56

Developing customer relations

Activity type and description	Delivery notes	Extra resources	Links to grading criteria	Links to student book
Outcome 2 Be able to apply appropriate presentation and interpersonal skills in customer service situations				
2.7 Introductory activity: Eat here?	Students are given an image of a person working in a restaurant. The presentation of the person and the restaurant are both poor, and students are asked to consider what is wrong.	Pens	P2	Pages 59–62
2.8 Worksheet: Self-evaluation	This questionnaire asks students to consider their own presentation by considering how often they iron their clothes, wash, etc. This should help them to realise the impression they may give to customers.	Worksheet on CD-ROM	P2	Pages 59–62
2.9 Worksheet: Body language	This worksheet gives students the chance to try and read body language. They are given six images to look at to try and read the body language of the situation.	Worksheet on CD-ROM	P2, M2	Pages 62–68
2.10 Worksheet: Are you listening?	This activity makes students listen and then repeat back what they have heard. Students should become aware of how much information they actually remember straight away and that listening is crucial if they are going to provide good customer service.	Worksheet on CD-ROM	M2	Pages 62–68
2.11 Discussion activity: Pardon?	These real-life scenarios allow students to think about the consequences of incorrect information or poor communication skills: how it affects customers' confidence in that service, and the impression that customers may have about future services.	Pen and paper	P2, M2	Pages 62–68
2.12 Discussion activity: Body piercings and tattoos	This activity asks students to discuss when body piercings and tattoos may be permitted and when they may not. They may be able to bring experience of stereotyping into the discussion and whether seeing tattoos and piercings on employees enhances or ruins the customer experience.	Pen and paper	P2	Pages 59–62
2.13 Plenary activity: Customer service (fishbone diagram)	This activity asks students to use a fishbone diagram to remember everything they have learned about customer service so far. The notes that they make by producing this diagram can be used to help write their assessed work.		P2	Pages 62–69

© Harcourt Education 2006

Activity type and description	Delivery notes	Extra resources	Links to grading criteria	Links to student book
2.14 Case study: The Dorchester Hotel in London	This case study looks at the range of customer services at the Dorchester Hotel in London and asks students to think about why customer service is so important in hotels.		P2	Pages 62–69
Outcome 3 Know how consistent and reliable customer service contributes to customer satisfaction				
2.15 Introductory activity: What do they mean?	This activity gives students the chance to think about what the words 'consistent' and 'reliable' mean, to help them with their assessed work for P3. They are asked to then apply what is meant by the two terms to various scenarios to help vocational learning of the concept.		P3	Pages 73–75
2.16 Worksheet: Work to do	This activity asks students to categorise activities according to how important or urgent they are in the customer service situation. This activity may also be extended to help students to practise their planning skills in other units.	Worksheet on CD-ROM	P3	Pages 73–75
2.17 Worksheet: Slogans	This activity gives students the chance to look at the impact of slogans on what customers expect of customer service from that product or business. This activity may also be used to consider consistency and reliability again, as, by buying products or services linked to these slogans, a customer gains an impression and expects a level of service.	Worksheet on CD-ROM, Internet access to look at companies	P3, also possibly towards M2	Pages 76–77
2.18 Discussion activity: Palm Court Hotel	Students are encouraged to consider the importance of customers who continue to keep staying at the same hotel year after year and the implications for the hotel of such customers, e.g. whether to make changes that these customers may like, how to satisfy customers in different ways when they keep returning, how to monitor their satisfaction, how to deal with any inconsistencies in service they may experience from year to year, etc.	Internet access to Palm Court site	P3, possibly D2	Pages 75–76

Developing customer relations

Activity type and description	Delivery notes	Extra resources	Links to grading criteria	Links to student book
2.19 Research activity: Service for internal customers	Consistent and reliable service is often talked about in terms of external customers, but this activity asks students to research what organisations do to help their internal customers, i.e. employees, by looking at the *Sunday Times* 100 Best Companies to Work For list. This list is updated each year, but students are referred in the first instance to the 2006 list. N.B. this list is accessible via www.timesonline.co.uk and www.bestcompanies.co.uk, and is unconnected with the Times100 websites.	Internet access	P3	Page 76
2.20 Case study: The Wow Awards	The Wow Awards website was set up by the Wow Group, led by Derek Williams. The website seeks to promote and award excellent customer service. Customers are invited to nominate businesses that do well. In this example students are given details about the Wow Award given to staff at The Present Finder Ltd. Students should be encouraged to visit the website and get details of the latest Wow Award nominations.	Internet access and paper	P3	Pages 73–77
2.21 Plenary activity: Customer satisfaction	Students are asked to mind-map seven points they have learned about how to satisfy customers on the diagram provided. These points can be used as part of their note-taking for assessed work.		P3	Pages 73–77
Outcome 4 Know how to monitor and evaluate customer service within an organisation				
2.22 Introductory activity: Customer comments book	This activity asks students to look at comments made in the customer comments book to make judgements about the different experiences that customers can have during different times of day. They are encouraged to think of ways to improve that service.		P4	Pages 79–81
2.23 Research activity: Customer satisfaction?	Students are asked to consider reviews of different hotels using www.holidaywatchdog.com and be able to consider the implications of differing customer reviews on their business.	Internet access	P4	Pages 79–82

© Harcourt Education 2006

Activity type and description	Delivery notes	Extra resources	Links to grading criteria	Links to student book
2.24 Worksheet: My class feedback	This activity asks students to think of five questions to ask fellow students about their experience with BTEC First Business this year. With teacher support, students can collect data and make constructive comments about what has gone well and any possible improvements for the future. Students should again become aware of how difficult it is to make sure all customers are satisfied all of the time!	Worksheet on CD-ROM, computer or paper to create questionnaire	P4, M3	Pages 79–82
2.25 Discussion activity: Employee feedback	This activity asks students to discuss times when they have been asked to give feedback to employers from a part-time job, work experience or even Student Satisfaction Survey. It can be an opportunity for them to think about how they felt giving opinions, their possible expectations of change at the end of it and the length/wording of the survey itself.	Notepaper	P4, M3	Pages 84–85
2.26 PowerPoint presentation: Monitoring customers	Different methods of collecting information are given in this presentation with an opportunity for the teacher to go through each method and ask students to consider the strengths of such methods and their limitations. This will help with the evaluation needed for Merit and Distinction work.	Ability to view PowerPoint	P4, M3, D2	Pages 79–84
2.27 Case study: Children's Express	Children's Express is a charity that monitors the opinions of children by reviewing products, services or news items. Such monitoring enables agencies, organisations and service providers to consider how they are received by children.	Internet access	P4	Pages 79–82
2.28 Case study: E-customer service	A survey by Transversal shows the different response times of organisations to email enquiries via websites in February 2005. Students are asked to consider the effect of these response times on monitoring and evaluating of customer comments, including the impression of customers accessing those websites.	Internet access	P4	Pages 79–82
2.29 Plenary activity: Monitoring customers	This activity asks students to write down all the methods of customer monitoring that they can think of, to revise and check their understanding of them. The more able students could extend the activity by judging, on the basis of their strengths and weaknesses, which ones are most effective, and then explain how those methods of monitoring and evaluation help the customer, business and employee.	Paper and pen	P4, M2	Pages 79–85

Unit 2 Activities

2.1 Introductory activity: What is customer service?

Student book pages 46–51

Look at the four different definitions of customer service given below.

- The degree of assistance and courtesy granted those who patronise the organisation. (www.customersurveystore.com/The_Process/Definitions/definitions.html)
- Quality of service delivery set by you or your department. (http://www1.umn.edu/ohr/trainingservices/sip/definitions.html)
- Customer services is the part of an organisation which answers customers' questions, exchanges goods which have been damaged, etc. (Cambridge Online Dictionary, http://dictionary.cambridge.org/)
- Customer Service is a function of how well an organisation meets the needs of its customers (http://www.customerservicepoint.com/customer-service-definition.html)

1 Which do you think is best, and why?
2 Which is most accurate, and why?
3 What is similar about them?
4 What is different about them?
5 If you want to challenge yourself – try and write one of your own!

2.2 Worksheet: Me as the customer

Student book pages 46–51

See CD-ROM

2.3 Worksheet: Customer needs

Student book pages 52–55

See CD-ROM

Outcome 1

© Harcourt Education 2006

2.4 Worksheet: Internal or external?

Student book pages 52–55

See CD-ROM

2.5 Research activity: Gathering data

Student book pages 52–55

Use this activity to help you make notes for your assessed piece of work. Write the name of the business that you are studying above the table, and then the details for each type of customer.

Business name:

Type of customer	Needs	Expectations

Outcome 1

2.6 Plenary activity: Right or wrong?

Student book pages 46–56

Is each of these responses right or wrong?

Scenario	Response	Is the response to the scenario right or wrong? What should have happened?
A customer comes back to a shop to return something. They don't have a receipt and it is company policy to only offer vouchers if no receipt is available. The customer is really angry and starts shouting and being aggressive.	The sales assistant gets very worried and starts panicking. They are afraid to tell their boss they find the customer difficult so they give a full cash refund.	
A wheel chair user is having trouble accessing items on the highest shelf.	A sales assistant walks past and asks if they need any assistance. They then offer to take them straight to the cash desk to pay.	
A woman is trying on a skirt and top in a changing room but is not able to get the right size.	The sales assistant is packing away clothes to be returned to the shop floor without noticing.	
A customer brings back a half-eaten ready meal saying there is an insect in it.	The sales assistant laughs and says they don't believe them.	
A big queue is developing and one of the cash desks runs out of till rolls.	The two assistants working either side chat about how badly supported they are at work and that there is never any till roll. The queue gets longer.	

Outcome 1

2.7 Introductory activity: Eat here?

Student book pages 59–62

What is wrong here?

2.8 Worksheet: Self-evaluation

Student book pages 59–62

See CD-ROM

2.9 Worksheet: Body language

Student book pages 62–68

See CD-ROM

2.10 Worksheet: Are you listening?

Student book pages 62–68

See CD-ROM

2.11 Discussion activity: Pardon?

Student book pages 62–68

These scenarios have both taken place in real life.

- A national television channel announced that a football game was to be played in Biarritz, northern Spain. Biarritz is in fact in France!
- A customer phoned up and tried to place a pizza order. The employee working in the restaurant spoke very little English and kept having to repeat the order over and over again. The call that should have taken one minute actually took six.

How do you think the customers of these services felt about it, and what are the implications for the provider?

2.12 Discussion activity: Body piercings and tattoos

Student book pages 59–62

In tattoo studios, hairdressers or beauty salons some members of staff are allowed to have tattoos or body piercings showing.

1. Discuss when you think it would not be appropriate to have such tattoos or piercings, and when it might be OK.
2. Are there any other fashions that you can think of that might not be suitable for the workplace?

2.13 Plenary activity: Customer service (fishbone diagram)

Student book pages 62–69

Finish the fishbone diagram by adding extra bones until you have made a note of everything you have learned about customer service.

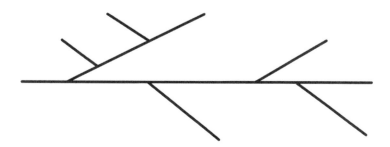

2.14 Case study: The Dorchester Hotel

Student book pages 62–69

Staff with an e-butler keyboard console

The Dorchester Hotel in London offers a range of facilities, including 'e-butlers' which are used to solve any IT problems for customers. A specially made console allows customers to access computer, printer, scanner, fax, DVD and CD facilities as well as watch television or read and send emails via a 42-inch plasma screen.

As well as these IT facilities, the hotel also offers the following services to its customers:

- 24-hour room service
- Air conditioning and heating throughout the hotel, all individually controlled
- Barber shop
- Car parking: limited space within hotel; close proximity to three public car parks
- Direct line fax machines
- E-butlers
- Hairdressing: Charles Worthington at The Dorchester Spa
- Wheelchair-accessible rooms
- In-house florist
- In-suite check-in
- ISDN lines
- Laundry, dry-cleaning and valet, with same-day service
- Luxury car service
- Medical service
- Mobile telephone rental
- Modems
- Multi-line telephones
- Non-smoking rooms
- Power supply; dual-voltage sockets
- Rooms/suites for guests with disabilities
- Suites for non-smokers
- Safe-deposit boxes
- Shopping gallery
- Theatre desk

1. Why do you think customer service is important in hotels?
2. What would happen to customer satisfaction if some of these services were not available?
3. Are there any services that you think should be added to this list to make the hotel even better?

Developing customer relations

2.15 Introductory activity: What do they mean?

Student book pages 73–75

As part of your assessment you are going to consider what consistent and reliable customer service is. So what do these words mean?

1. Write down the first meaning that you can think of…

Consistent means
Reliable means

2. Now apply what is meant by consistent and reliable to these services or products received by customers. What do customers need for it to be consistent? What do customers need for it to be reliable?

Service or product	Consistent means … Reliable means …
Having a haircut	
Travelling by plane	
Downloading music from a website	
Clothing bought in the same shop	
A cleaner keeping a director's office clean	

Outcome 3

2.16 Worksheet: Work to do

Student book pages 73–75

See CD-ROM

2.17 Worksheet: Slogans

Student book pages 76–77

See CD-ROM

2.18 Discussion activity: Palm Court Hotel

Student book pages 75–76

The Palm Court Hotel in Malta states that it has customers who have returned to the hotel more than 40 consecutive times.

1. How important do you think customers returning is to a hotel like Palm Court?
2. What might Palm Court have to do to keep these types of customers satisfied?

For more information on the Palm Court Hotel, visit www.palmcourtmalta.com

---

2.19 Research activity: Service for internal customers

Student book page 76

Using the website www.timesonline.co.uk or www.bestcompanies.co.uk, look up the 100 best companies to work for. Look at the services that two of the companies provide for their employees.

1. Which services do they offer their employees?
2. How do they try and satisfy their employees?
3. How do they measure success? Share your opinions with the class.

Developing customer relations 45

2.20 Case study: The Wow Awards

Student book pages 73–77

The Wow Awards (www.thewowawards.co.uk) are given by people wanting to nominate and reward organisations for really good customer service. A recent example on the website has been that of the staff at The Present Finder Ltd who gave excellent customer service to a customer.

Alison Hall had ordered several items for Christmas from The Present Finder and they all arrived on time.

Unfortunately one of them was broken and, when she emailed to get a replacement, it was out of stock. To make up for this the company offered an immediate refund and sent a prepaid label to return the item.

Alison chose to have the item replaced and was sent free chocolates as well.

This shows how a bad situation was made good to the point that she even felt The Present Finder should get a Wow Award – this shows excellent customer service!

1 Give two ways in which The Present Finder gave good customer service.
2 How important was it to make Alison feel that her problem was sorted out?
3 How did they exceed her expectations and make her feel really satisfied with her service?

2.21 Plenary activity: Customer satisfaction

Student book pages 73–77

On the diagram below, against each of the branches, write ways in which customers can be satisfied. You can use these to help you with your assessed work.

Outcome 3 © Harcourt Education 2006

2.22 Introductory activity: Customer comments book

Student book pages 79–81

Look at the copy of the customer comments book, and in pairs or small groups discuss what you would do if you were manager of this restaurant to make sure the service was reliable and consistent.

Date and time	Comment
7 August 7.45 am	Excellent food and very well cooked. No queue at all so I was able to get on my journey quickly. Michelle took my order carefully and made me very welcome.
7 August 8.00 am	My family and I really enjoyed our breakfast, we will come again
7 August 8.15 am	Excellent service and well prepared even though they were busy. John worked very hard. Congratulations to the chef! My only criticism is that £8.00 for breakfast seems a bit expensive.
7 August 8.30 am	Too slow – couldn't wait, decided to go elsewhere. Only one waitress serving and the chef couldn't keep up with the orders.
7 August 8.35 am	Very nice food even if a bit slow. Maybe you should think about getting more staff
7 August 8.40 am	Totally agree with customer above – 45 minute wait is too long – please get more staff.
7 August 9.00 am	Didn't have to wait long at all – keep up the good work.
7 August 11.00 am	Very nice tea and cake – will definitely come back again – thanks Michelle.
7 August 12.30 pm	Waiting time of 40 minutes is too long for lunch – please sort this out or I won't be coming back
7 August 12.45 pm	Too expensive, long wait, dirty tables – yuk – wont come back here again!
7 August 1.30 pm	Thanks to Michelle and the team for really good service again – you all deserve a pay rise

Developing customer relations   47

2.23 Research activity: Customer satisfaction?

Student book pages 79–82

No two people ever experience exactly the same level of customer service, as their expectations of what they should receive are different.

Websites like www.holidaywatchdog.com allow customers to give their own opinions about what they think of a holiday destination. This is one way of getting customer feedback to the hotels that receive the comments, but the feedback may also add to or damage the reputation of that business. Access the website and look at three reviews for the same hotel of your choice.

1 How are the reviews similar?
2 How are they different?
3 Are there any improvements or changes that the hotel should make?
4 What effect might these reviews have on the reputation of the hotel?

2.24 Worksheet: My class feedback

Student book pages 79–82

See CD-ROM

2.25 Discussion activity: Employee feedback

Student book pages 84–85

As well as getting feedback from external customers, many organisations are now very interested in getting feedback from their internal customers (employees) about how they feel about their organisation. In small groups, discuss any employee feedback that you have experienced in your part-time job or work experience.

1 What kind of questions were you asked?
2 What happened to the information?
3 What did it feel like to be asked your opinion?

Your college or school may have also carried out a Student Satisfaction Survey, so you may be able to use your experience of this as well.

2.26 PowerPoint presentation: Monitoring customers

Student book pages 79–84

See CD-ROM

2.27 Case study: Children's Express

Student book pages 79–82

Children's Express is a website that asks children to review products and news, and to make comments in general to improve their lives. As a charity Children's Express can give feedback and comments to all sorts of businesses and organisations about how products or services are seen by children, and any possible changes that they should make.

Reviews have been provided on all aspects of life, from political or legal change such as the introduction of ASBOs, to which fast-food chain has the best vegetarian burger.

Access www.childrens-express.org and see the latest reports that are affecting children today.

How can their comments be used to improve products and services received from profit and not-for-profit organisations?

Developing customer relations 49

2.28 Case study: E-customer service

Student book pages 79–82

In February 2005 Transversal, an e-customer service monitoring agency, monitored the amount of time that different organisations took to answer email enquiries. They found that 44 per cent of those emails went unanswered, and that those that were answered took an average of 33 hours to be answered!

From the sample of organisations used, the shortest time to answer the emails came from banking organisations, which answered 60 per cent of emails in an average time of 17 hours. 40 per cent of emails were not answered!

Travel organisations only responded to 40 per cent of emails in an average time of 42 hours. 60 per cent of emails were not answered!

This survey carried out by Transversal in 2005 and published on the www.ecustomerserviceworld.com website shows the different levels of customer service between different types of organisation.

1. What impression might customers get of these times to answer emails?
2. Why is it important to answer emails about e-services as soon as possible?
3. How might this affect the monitoring and evaluation of customer service?

2.29 Plenary activity: Monitoring customers

Student book pages 79–85

In pairs, write down all of the different ways that you have learned during this unit to monitor customer comments and complaints. Put them in order of which methods you think are best and give reasons why. Share your opinions with other pairs of students in your class.

Unit 2 Exemplar assignment

Assignment 2.4

Background to the assignment

For this assignment you will need to continue to carry out research by visit or collecting information in newspapers or websites on British Airways. Add this work to the rest of your portfolio for Unit 2 on British Airways. Use information on www.ba.com and the class handouts to help you.

This assignment aims to help you achieve:

P4 Describe how customer service can be monitored and evaluated

M3 Explain how monitoring and evaluating can improve customer service for the customer, the organisation and the employee

D2 Analyse, using examples, how effective customer service benefits the customer, the organisation and the employee.

Remember to include a bibliography at the end of your work with a list of all the websites you have used, and clearly show information that you have collected from websites or text books, with the author or site shown in brackets.

Task 1 (P4)

Describe how customer service can be monitored and evaluated

For this task you will firstly need to produce a table (as below) giving details about how British Airways actually monitor and evaluate their customers –

for **monitoring**, how they make use of:

- informal customer feedback
- customer questionnaires/comment cards
- staff feedback
- mystery customers
- complaints/customer letters

for **evaluating**, how they make judgements about customer service based on:

- level of sales (think about whether sales are increasing or decreasing due to customer service)
- repeat customers (customers who are returning to the business again and again)
- new customers
- level of complaints/compliments
- staff turnover (the number of staff leaving or joining the business)

Method of monitoring	Explanation	How British Airways use this type of feedback	What evidence British Airways could use to make judgements about it

Task 2 (M3)

Explain how monitoring and evaluating can improve customer service for the customer, the organisation and the employee.

To work towards Merit you will need to explain how this monitoring and evaluating helps

- the customer
- the organisation
- the employee

and produce a presentation to be given to your group.

For each of these different groups, think about the effect on the

- quality of service
- reliability
- improved services
- keeping staff
- getting new customers
- increasing sales
- keeping in line with the law
- better conditions for employees.

Task 3 (D2)

Analyse, using examples, how effective customer service benefits the customer, the organisation and the employee

If you wish to work towards Distinction you will need to give examples of customer service and look at the benefits and limitations of customer service.

Student's work

Task 1

Task 1

Method of monitoring	Explanation	How British Airways use this type of feedback	What evidence British Airways could use to make judgements about it
Informal customer feedback (External)	Informal Customer Feedback means the type of comments that customers might make when they are waiting for a flight or sitting in an airport. This feedback is passed on to staff and they can suggest changes that could be made to their supervisors. The supervisors then make the suggestions to the managers so that they can improve services.	British Airways have used Customer Feedback to make changes to their services such as online check-in. This means that customers giving feedback about having to wait in queues to book their seat were listened to and so online check-in was introduced so that customers could print their own boarding pass and choose their own seat.	British Airways sales have been increasing over the past x years and in May 2006 they had made £620 million profit and had increased their numbers of customers and BA said that lots of these customers were in Business Class and First Class. This shows that they are getting more customers than before so they must be getting new and repeat customers to buy their tickets. There are also more customers in general wanting to travel by plane. www.timesonline.co.uk

Developing customer relations

Student's work

Task 1

Method of monitoring	Explanation	How British Airways use this type of feedback	What evidence British Airways could use to make judgements about it
Customer questionnaires/comment cards (External)	A customer questionnaire or comment card is a way of asking customers different questions about what they think about the service that is offered. This may be done online via a website, by telephone or on paper.	British Airways use all three different methods of gaining customer feedback. They use questionnaires on websites to ask customers about their services and whether or not they would choose to fly with them. British Airways also give out questionnaires to passengers to fill out during the flights. This means that they can give an immediate idea about what they think. The questionnaires are given out and collected by Cabin Crew. Sometimes British Airways employ agencies to collect information about their services and they ring existing and new customers to ask them what they think about the services and then BA make changes or listen to their customers.	British Airways ask 48,000 people on their planes every month to tell them about how they are doing. They use the answers from these questionnaires to make changes so they can judge whether or not customers like the food or about the way that the airport lounge is organised www.britishairways.com
Staff feedback (Internal)	Staff feedback is information that is provided by employees about their jobs or about different ways of improving the service that they give to customers. Staff are internal customers so they can give their views about how they feel to work for the organisation through something like an employee survey or monitoring	At British Airways staff are able to give feedback individually or through their union. The Transport and General Workers union supports employees as a group to make changes to the way they work. British Airways can monitor how staff feel supported by looking at surveys given on their staff.	British Airways have given all their staff a £48 million bonus to be shared out in May 2005 based on the good profits they had made. This is likely to make them happy. British Airways have also been voted in the top 100 employers supporting employees who are lesbian or gay by Stonewall in 2005.

Exemplar assignment © Harcourt Education 2006

Task 1

Method of monitoring	Explanation	How British Airways use this type of feedback	What evidence British Airways could use to make judgements about it
Mystery customers (External)	A mystery customer is one that is not known to staff. They are someone who is using the services of the customer in order to give feedback to the business as if they are a real customer. At the end of the experience the mystery customer gives a report to British Airways giving them information about the experience.	British Airways use mystery customers to given them feedback. The mystery customer gives them ratings on the service, food and so on. The information can they be used by British Airways to improve their services.	British Airways will get reports from their Mystery Shopping Agency and they tell them what is happening and how customers feel. This helps them to make a judgement about whether or not they feel customer service is getting better and if they need to make any more changes.
Complaints/ customer letters (External)	Customer letters and customer complaints are a good way to work out if there is a common problem happening within the business. Some businesses will code different complaints for example in to wrong size, wrong quality, did not meet expectations and so on. This means that they can use the data to see if there is a pattern forming about what makes customers annoyed or upset. The same is true of customer letters that are saying good things about the service. Good comments given by customers about staff or services can be used to reward staff eg employee of the month or used to make staff feel valued	British Airways use their complaints and customer letters to work out different ways to improve their service or make adjustments. They may decide to stop flying to a particular airport if there are complaints about or they may introduce extra services on particular flights eg on longer flights passengers are given their own individual television screen with a choice of up to 10 films to choose from. It is likely that this came as a result of customers wanting a wider choice of films.	British Airways get 70,000 comment cards from their passengers every year. That is quite a lot. They use the information to help them make things better.

Task 2

Slide 1

British Airways Customer Service

Slide 2

Customers

- Monitoring and making judgements about customer services helps customers of BA because
- BA can make changes for them eg food or times
- They may find travelling or buying a ticket easier eg online
- The planes should be more likely to be reliable for them as BA want to please customers

Slide 3

BA

- Monitoring and making judgements about customer services helps BA because
- They can keep customers happy so they will come back so they make more money
- They can provide a better service so people think of flying with them
- They can spend less time sorting out complaints because they are doing better

Slide 4

Employees

- Monitoring and making judgements about customer service helps employees of BA because
- If more external customers are happy their job is likely to be easier and they will feel happy
- If employees know that they are listened to they may feel happier in their jobs
- They are likely to have better conditions for their work so they are safer and healthier at work eg monitoring their hours at work.
- They might get another bonus like in May 2006 if the business keeps making more profit.

For Tasks 1 and 2

Assessor feedback

You have produced some really good work for P4 – your table is really very good and you have thought a lot about how British Airways can monitor and evaluate different types of customers. You have given used lots of evidence that you have collected from websites and from newspapers, so well done but make sure you add a bibliography at the end of your portfolio to explain where you got these figures from.

You have also produced a good presentation for M3 with some judgements about how British Airways could improve customer service for the customer, themselves and employees by monitoring and evaluating. The witness statement I have added shows that you have achieved M3 by thinking about issues such as reliability, quality of service and so on for this unit.

If you wish to improve this work to D2 level you will need to go back through your work and think of specific examples when BA has demonstrated effective customer service and how this has benefited the customer, organisation and employee. You will need to analyse the examples so you will need to look not only at the really positive implications of that benefit but also the limitations of that benefit, for one of the other groups, for example.

A customer service benefit might be that BA is offering customers a better online service. This benefits the customer, as it is more convenient, and the organisation because it is cheaper, but may not benefit employees as it is likely that less staff would be needed, so they may be worried about their jobs.

You will need to think of examples like this and analyse these customer service benefits in lots of detail.

For Task 2 PowerPoint presentation

Witness Statement for Sarah Smith

Presentation on British Airways

Explaining how British Airways use monitoring and evaluating to improve customer service.

Sarah you gave a very good presentation on how British Airways monitoring and evaluating customer service helps the customer, organisation and employees.

You made good references to appropriate examples such as the way that British Airways can improve the customer experience by changing their facilities or food so that the customer has a good experience.

You also gave further examples for the organisation itself and employees. Although you did not add them as a heading to a slide you were also able to think back to your work for P4 and talk about the role of unions when helping to think about how employees could be consulted and the way that British Airways works with them.

Well done.

Unit 2 Resources

Additional resources that can be used to support student learning of this Unit are:

Textbooks

Carysforth, C. and Neild, M., *BTEC First Business* (Heinemann, 2006)

Bee, F. and Bee, R., *Customer Care* (Chartered Institute of Personnel and Development, 1999)

Hayes, J. and Dredge, F., *Managing Customer Service* (Gower Publishing, 1998)

Johns, T. *Perfect Customer Care* (Arrow Business Books, 1999)

Dransfield, R. *et al.*, *BTEC National Business: Student Book* (Heinemann, 2004). This resource may be useful for those students operating at Distinction level who require additional information to help them.

Websites

www.bized.ac.uk   Bized business education site

Unit 3 Investigating financial control

Unit overview

Unit 3 is a specialist unit for the BTEC First Certificate and a core unit of the BTEC First Diploma qualifications in Business. The unit gives students practical and theoretical information about the way that finances are used within the business world.

Students are given an introduction to the world of costs and revenues, and what is meant by profit, in order to be able to use analyses such as break even to work out acceptable levels of output for a business to survive.

Cash flow forecasting is also examined so that students can appreciate the concept of money going in to and out of a business in terms of the ability of a business to pay its bills. The idea that a profitable business can go out of business due to cash flow problems is also explored.

Finally the unit considers business transactions and the methods that organisations use to record different transactions including the way that fraud may be detected and prevented in order to protect the business from losing money in this way.

Suggested activities

The table on the following pages shows how activities in this Assessment and Delivery Resource cover the four different outcomes of the Unit. There are a variety of tasks including discussion material, worksheets, case studies and presentation material.

The research tasks have been prepared to allow students to gather evidence in note form to help them produce their own work.

How this unit will be assessed

To gain a Pass, learners will need to:

P1 describe, using examples, the importance of costs, revenue and profit for a business organisation

P2 calculate break-even using given data to show the level at which income equals expenditure

P3 prepare an annual cash flow forecast using monthly data

P4 describe simple ways of recording financial transactions and preventing fraud in a business organisation.

To gain a Merit requires learners to complete all the Pass requirements plus the Merit requirements, where they need to:

M1 demonstrate the impact of changing cost and revenue data on the break even point of a selected business

M2 analyse the implications of regular and irregular cash inflows and outflows for a business organisation.

To gain a Distinction requires a learner to complete all the Pass and Merit requirements plus the Distinction requirements, where they need to:

D1 evaluate how cash flows and financial recording systems can contribute to managing business finances.

Learning outcomes

The unit is based on the following learning outcomes

1. Understand the costs, revenue and profit for a business operation
2. Know how businesses use break even analysis
3. Be able to prepare a cash flow forecast
4. Understand ways of recording financial transactions.

At-a-glance

Activity type and description	Delivery notes	Extra resources	Links to grading criteria	Links to textbook
Outcome 1 Understand the costs, revenue and profit for a business operation				
3.1 Introductory activity: Bob's Removals	This activity gives students the chance to see what impact a change in the price of fuel may have on the variable costs of a removal business. This could be linked into current information about fuel prices and initiate discussion on how oil price increases affect everyone.	News articles, websites	P1, P2	Pages 90–92
3.2 Worksheet: Which type of cost?	This sorting activity allows students to consider which costs are fixed, variable and start up costs. It may be useful to also transfer these different costs on to card so that students can sort them into piles to use.	Worksheet on CD-ROM. Cards if required	P1	Pages 90–92
3.3 Discussion activity: Which business is performing best?	Comparing the different gross and net profit figures for three businesses gives students the chance to consider the importance of each.		P1, P2	Pages 92–96
3.4 Plenary activity: What is profit for?	An activity that asks students to label six different ways profit can be used. This activity can be extended by also considering the concept of opportunity cost.		P1	Pages 94–96
Outcome 2 Know how businesses use break-even analysis				
3.5 Worksheet: Break-even chart	A half-completed break-even chart is presented to students for them to finish by labelling all the appropriate sections. They are also asked to consider what would happen if fixed costs increased and the affect on the BEP.	Worksheet on CD-ROM	P2, M1	Pages 99–103
3.6 Case study: Redtown FC	An activity that asks students to produce a break-even chart for a small football club and then the impact that a change in price would have on the break even point.	Calculators	P2, M1	Pages 99–103

Activity type and description	Delivery notes	Extra resources	Links to grading criteria	Links to textbook
3.7 Plenary activity: True or false quiz	A true or false activity that can be used as a starter or plenary activity.		P2	Pages 99–105
Outcome 3 Be able to prepare a cash flow forecast				
3.8 Introductory activity: Cash inflow and cash outflow	This exercise asks students to consider whether a list of items represent money coming in or money going out.		P3	Pages 108–111
3.9 Discussion activity: Going bust?	Considering the number of businesses and people who go into liquidation or file for personal bankruptcy puts the issue of cash flow into context. This activity is extended to ask students to make recommendations about how such events could be avoided.	Websites, news articles	P3, M2	Pages 111–116
3.10 Research/discussion activity: Cash-flow forecasting	A practical cash-flow activity for students to use for practice. This activity is extended by asking students to make recommendations about the situation of this business and ways to improve it.		P3, M2	Pages 111–116
3.11 Case study: Business advisor	A completed cash-flow forecast is given for students to write a report on. They need to give details about what is happening by considering improvements that could be made and access to finance.		P3, M2, D1	Pages 111–116
Outcome 4 Understand ways of recording financial transactions				
3.12 Introductory activity: Which is which?	Definitions of different types of paperwork are given and students are asked to match the type of paperwork to the definition provided.		P4	Pages 119–121

Activity type and description	Delivery notes	Extra resources	Links to grading criteria	Links to textbook
3.13 Research activity: College canteen	An simple activity designed to allow students to follow the path of an item that has been bought in the canteen, e.g. the purchase order that was used to order it, goods received note, etc., and the way fraud could be prevented at each of the stages of recording.	Whiteboard. Card or paper to allow students to draw their findings	P4	Pages 129–133
3.14 Worksheet: Fraud	Students consider different types of payments and list different methods of dealing with fraud, based on their own experience, or methods they have heard of.	Worksheet on CD-ROM. Internet access, newspapers, magazines	P4	Pages 133–136
3.15 Case study: Happy Mondays?	A disorganised business person is not keeping effective records of their business, Students are asked to spot the errors and make recommendations for how they should be improved, and to measure the impact on the business.		P4, D1	Pages 119–133
3.16 PowerPoint presentation: Fraud	This PowerPoint presentation deals with all aspects of fraud and makes students aware of some of the methods of prevention and the impact on business and themselves. It makes links with websites, so this activity can be extended with Internet access.	Projector, Internet access	P4	Pages 133–136

Unit 3 Activities

3.1 Introductory activity: Bob's Removals

Student book pages 90–92

Bob runs a removal business. His fixed costs are the same each week and are set at £400 per week. The only variable cost he must pay for is fuel for his van. Over four weeks he uses the following amount of petrol in litres:

Week	Petrol used, in litres
Week 1	200
Week 2	500
Week 3	800
Week 4	500

1. Work out how much his fuel costs would be if the price is 79 pence per litre.
2. Fuel prices are rumoured to be going up to as high as 99 pence per litre:
    a. What effect could that have on his variable costs for four weeks like those shown above?
    b. Would could this mean for his customers?
    c. What could he do to avoid this?

3.2 Worksheet: Which type of cost?

Student book pages 90–92

See CD-ROM

3.3 Discussion activity: Which business is performing the best?

Student book pages 92–96

Each of these businesses buys and sells clothing. The only variable costs they have are for buying the stock to sell. All other costs are fixed. All costs and revenues are shown per week.

Item	Snappy Fashions £	Chic Boutique £	Tall and Small £
Fixed costs	500	600	800
Variable costs	300	400	600
Revenue	900	1200	1000

1. Using the figures provided, work out the gross profit and net profit for each business.
2. Which business has the best gross profit?
3. Which one has the best net profit?
4. What do each of them mean and which is most important?
5. Why should a business make sure that it is careful when monitoring its fixed and variable costs?

3.4 Plenary activity: What is profit for?

Student book pages 94–96

Profit is really important to a business, and can be used in a variety of ways.

Profits

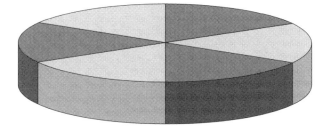

1. Label each of the six sections given below with different ways that profit can be used.
2. What happens if one of these sections receives more of the profit than other sections?
3. What could this mean for the business?

Outcome 1 © Harcourt Education 2006

3.5 Worksheet: Break-even chart

Student book pages 99–103

See CD-ROM

3.6 Case study: Redtown FC

Student book pages 99–103

Redtown FC is a local football team aiming to go into Conference League next season.

- Their ground has capacity for 5,000 people to watch the games.
- They play 25 home games every season.
- They have an admission charge to everyone of £7 per game.
- At the moment the club gets 3,000 people watching each home game.
- The club has the costs shown in the table, which must be paid each season, covering all of the 20 home games.
- The club has to pay the local police a fee of £2 per spectator to cover policing.

Costs	£
Insurance	21,000
Players' wages	60,000
Office staff	36,000
Heating and lighting	16,000
Ground staff	12,000
Stewards	6,000
Printing and publicity	9,000

The club is thinking about reducing the price of each ticket to £5 per game to encourage more people to watch the games next season. What impact would this have on the break-even point?

3.7 Plenary activity: True or false?

Student book pages 99–105

Say which of these statements are true and which are false.

- BEP stands for Break Equal Point.
- If fixed costs rise and variable costs stay the same, a business must sell more to break even.
- Reducing the selling price will lower the break-even point.
- A break-even chart can predict the number of sales you are going to make.
- The margin of safety is the number of units of sales that a business can fall by before it reaches the break-even point.
- Revenue means the amount of profit a business is going to make.
- When using the BEP you round up to the nearest whole product if the answer is 0.4 of a product.
- The formula for working out BEP is:

$$BEP = \frac{FC}{SP - VC}$$

3.8 Introductory activity: Cash inflow and cash outflow

Student book pages 108–111

Look through this list and tick whether they are cash inflows or outflows.

Item	Cash inflow	Cash outflow
Business rates		
Cash sales		
Credit sales		
Heating and lighting		
Interest payments		
Loan		
Maintenance		
Stock to sell		
Telephone		
Transport fees		
Wages		

3.9 Discussion activity: Going bust?

Student book pages 111–116

It was suggested that there were 3,439 companies going in to liquidation between January and March 2006. This represented a 17% increase compared to the same time in the first three months of 2005.

People announcing they were personally bankrupt also went up during 2006, and this was said to be due to people wanting to buy now and worry about payment later.

1. What does bankrupt mean?
2. What does liquidation mean?
3. In small groups, work out how good cash flow management could help reduce the chances of a business going in to liquidation.
4. As a group, agree three recommendations that you would make to businesses so that they avoid going in to liquidation.
5. As a group, agree three recommendations that you would make to individuals about what they should do to avoid having money problems and becoming personally bankrupt.

Outcome 3

Investigating financial control 67

3.10 Research/discussion activity: Cash-flow forecasting

Student book pages 111–116

1. Using the table below, see if you can draw up a cash-flow forecast.
   - The bank balance in January was £200
   - Receipts from customers were £800 (Jan), £1000 (Feb) and £1500 (Mar)
   - £650 was spent on premises only in January
   - £100 was spent on equipment in January
   - Gas and electric bills were £75 in total every month
   - Wages were £500 per month
   - Payments to suppliers were £300 per month.

	Jan	**Feb**	**Mar**
Opening balance			
Receipts from customers			
Total receipts			
Cash outflows			
• Premises			
• Equipment			
• Energy			
• Wages			
• Suppliers			
Total payments			
Closing balance			

2. How are things going for this business?
3. How could its cash flow be improved?

Outcome 3

3.11 Case study: Business advisor

Student book pages 111–116

Look at the cash-flow forecast given to you below for Shannon's business. She sells cakes and pastries in a small shop in her town.

	May	June	July	Aug	Sep	Oct
	£	£	£	£	£	£
Opening bank balance	500	–4,800	–6,000	–6,100	–6,200	–6,500
Receipts						
Loan	5,000	0	0	0	0	0
Cash sales	0	800	1,200	800	1,000	800
Credit sales	0	0	600	1,000	600	800
Total receipts	5,000	800	1,800	1,800	1,600	1,600
Payments						
Purchases of stock	4,000	800	800	800	800	800
Wages	1,000	1,000	1,000	1,000	1,000	1,000
Telephone bills	300	200	100	100	100	100
Shop and fixtures	5,000	0	0	0	0	0
Total payments	10,300	2,000	1,900	1,900	1,900	1,900
Closing bank balance	–4,800	–6,000	–6,100	–6,200	–6,500	–6,800

Write a short report to Shannon about what is happening to her business at the moment.

Explain each of the areas of the cash flow forecast to her and tell her what this cash-flow forecast shows.

Make recommendations to her about what she should do to try and improve this cash-flow forecast by giving her reasons why cash flows are so important to her business, and what happens to her business if she does not manage them carefully.

Consider her:

- borrowing
- credit facilities
- preparation for emergencies/ability to pay her bills.

Investigating financial control 69

3.12 Introductory activity: Which is which?

Student book pages 119–121

To help you remember the different types of paperwork that you need to think about for this unit, match the correct definition to the type of paperwork in the table below. They are all mixed up for you to find.

Paperwork		Definition
Cash receipt		A summary of the account with a slip or advice note for payment
Cheque or electronic transfer		Gives details of how much needs to be paid for goods
Credit note		Lists items that have been brought in to the business
Delivery note		Lists items to be ordered
Goods received note		Money back if anything is returned or charged too much for
Purchase order		Note given to show payment has been made by cash
Remittance advice		Sent with items as proof they have been sent
Sales invoice		Summarises everything for that organisation including how much money they owe
Statement of account		Way of paying for goods

3.13 Research activity: College canteen

Student book pages 129–133

Every day you go to your college shop or canteen and make payments for items that you buy there.

1. Draw a chart showing the path of an item that you buy in one of these locations. Trace the item to all the places where it is recorded, from the cash register, through to the departments of the college where you are, and on to the Accounts Department. What happens to it there?

2. For each part of the transaction, name the appropriate type of paperwork that goes with the recording of the transaction, e.g. Goods Received Note when it was brought in to the college, Invoice to pay for it, and all the other stages before you could buy the item.

3. How could fraud be prevented at each of these stages?

Outcome 4

3.14 Worksheet: Fraud

Student book pages 133–136

See CD-ROM

3.15 Case study: Happy Mondays?

Student book pages 119–133

Look through this case study and see how many mistakes Mr Monday is making in his business.

Mr Monday ran his own gardening business. He really enjoyed dealing with the customers and was happy to spend time talking to them. As his business was only a small enterprise he didn't see the point of having a cash register to take money from sales. He kept the money in a drawer in his desk under a pile of books, because he had lost the key ages ago.

His invoices were kept in a file labelled Invoices but they were all out of order, and he often forgot to file them. This meant that sometimes he even forgot to pay them, but luckily his suppliers knew he was a bit absent-minded so they would telephone and remind him when he owed them money. He didn't bother to check the amount he sent them and any goods that he ordered were put at the front of the shop ready to be put away eventually. As customers often distracted him he was never quite sure where they went.

Mr Monday always telephoned through any orders, roughly estimating what he thought he had sold. This meant from time to time he had too many of one plant or another, and he then sold them off quickly as part of a sale or special offer.

If someone came in to pay by cheque for goods he would ask them to write their name and address on the back of the cheque, just in case he needed them, but these details would be lost once he paid them in to the bank. Mr Monday had seen three cheques returned to him by the bank in the last four months, and he was wondering why that was happening.

Mr Monday had received a number of letters from the Inland Revenue asking him to make a tax return for his business. He had filed those somewhere and thought he would get round to doing them one day.

1. What should he be doing?
2. What would you advise him to do first?

3.16 PowerPoint presentation: Fraud

Student book pages 133–136

See CD-ROM

Unit 3 Exemplar assignment

Assignment 3.3: Cash flow management

Assignment background

This assignment provides evidence for Unit 3 by asking you to produce a cash flow forecast for a new horse-riding business.

P3 Prepare an annual cash flow forecast using monthly data.

M2 Analyse the implications of regular and irregular cash inflows and outflows for a business organisation.

You have been asked to prepare an annual cash flow forecast for a new horse-riding stables business opening in town called Hot to Trot that is being opened by your friend Jayne Styles. She is going to provide riding lessons for children and adults in the local area by renting buildings from a local farmer. Within this assignment you have two tasks to prepare:

Task 1 (P3)

Cash flow forecast

Using the figures Jayne has written down below,

1. produce a cash flow forecast for the next 12 months.
2. explain what the cash flow forecast shows.

Task 2 (M2)

Regular inflows and outflows

Using the cash flow forecast you have produced for Hot to Trot, analyse the implications of regular and irregular inflows and outflows, to show, using examples:

1. what effect a regular flow of money into and out of a business will have on profitability.
2. what would happen if money did not flow in to the business regularly, or if Hot to Trot did not make outflows regularly.

Hot to Trot

Hot to Trot is to be opened on 3 March.

Expected number of lessons to be given a week – 400 lessons per month maximum – although during the first 6 months this will need to build up. Estimated – Month 1: 40; Month 2: 80; Month 3: 160; Month 4: 220; Month 5: 280; and from then on 400 per month until December when for three months it is expected that lessons will reduce to 200 per month due to the colder weather.

Lessons are to be charged at £20 per hour.

Feed for the horses is expected to be £400 per month and Jayne has two months to pay her supplier two months in arrears. The horses are due to arrive at the stables in February.

Vets expenses of around £150 per month from February onwards.

Insurance will be £500 per month.

There are two options for payment: Half of the lessons are offered for immediate payment and students are to give their cash at the start of the lesson, the other half of the lessons allow students to pay one month in arrears.

The business will start with £10 000 that will be put into its bank account on 1 February. Jayne has also been promised a bank loan of £10 000 that will be put in to the account on 1 April, and from 1 May she will need to pay it back at £250 per month.

The stables need renovation before they can open and the cost of these is £5000. The work is due to be carried out in February, with opening in March.

The business estimates spending £10 000 on the horses and equipment needed for them in February – the equipment includes tack (saddles, bridles, reins, head collars, etc.), grooming tools, blankets, haynets and so on.

The energy bill is expected to be £6 000 per year and the business expects to pay it bills at the end of each quarter which is every three months starting in June.

The wage bill is expected to be £2 000 per month starting in February.

Telephone expenses are estimated to be £600 for the year and the business will pay its bill monthly, starting in March.

The rent to the farmer for using his buildings and grazing land is £300 per month for the first year and, as he is keen to support the business, he has agreed to only start charging after the opening on 3 March. This charge includes a charge for water.

Jayne has decided to take out an advert in a local magazine for 6 months starting in March to advertise her service. The cost per month is £75.

James Day

Task 1: Cash flow Forecast for Hot to Trot

The cash flow forecast on the following page for Jayne shows that she is going to have a loss until August and then she is going to make a profit after that.

Tasks 1 and 2

Task 2

Inflows mean the money that comes in to the business and outflow means the money going out of the business. Jayne has got some regular payments going out of the business so these are regular outflows. These are things like rent, wages and telephone. Jayne knows these are going to be paid out of the business. For inflows she has regular inflows because she is being paid for lessons every month. She is going to make a lot of profit from the inflows because by September she is going to be making money.

> **Assessor feedback**
>
> **James you have produced a really good cash flow forecast for Task 1 that does show that you can produce an annual cash flow forecast for a business. Your explanation that goes with it does need to be given more clearly before I can fully award you P1.**
>
> **A cash flow forecast shows the amount of money going into a business – inflows and the amount of money going out of a business – outflows. These amounts of money are used by the business to show times when they are going to find it easier to make their payments and times when they may have difficulty so they might need to get an overdraft or loan to help. A cash flow forecast is not designed to show profit and loss and the closing and opening balances actually show the amount of money that Jayne has in her bank rather than the amount of profit she has made. Use the BTEC First Book for Unit 3 to help you with this concept if you need to.**
>
> **For M2 you have started to consider the inflows and outflows but you have not added enough detail. You will need to consider regular inflows for Jayne and irregular inflows. You will also need to write out regular outflows and irregular outflows. Analysis means what do they mean for the business – how do they help the business, what are the consequences for the business of them? Use examples to help with this as much as possible.**

Task 1

James Day — Task 1: Cash flow Forecast for Hot to Trot

	Feb £	Mar £	Apr £	May £	Jun £	Jul £	Aug £	Sep £	Oct £	Nov £	Dec £	Jan £
Opening balance	10000	−8200	−11375	−4150	−5975	−6400	−5625	−3050	800	4650	8500	12350
Loan			10000									
Cash Payments	0	400	800	1600	2200	2800	4000	4000	4000	4000	4000	2000
Credit Payments	0	0	400	800	1600	2200	2800	4000	4000	4000	4000	4000
Total Receipts	0	400	11200	2400	3800	5000	6800	8000	8000	8000	8000	6000
Cash outflows												
Renovation	5000	0	0	0	0	0	0	0	0	0	0	0
Horse Equipment	10000	0	0	0	0	0	0	0	0	0	0	0
Horse Feed Suppliers	0	0	400	400	400	400	400	400	400	400	400	400
Energy Bill	500	500	500	500	500	500	500	500	500	500	500	500
Vet Bills	150	150	150	150	150	150	150	150	150	150	150	150
Insurance	500	500	500	500	500	500	500	500	500	500	500	500
Loan Interest	0	0	0	250	250	250	250	250	250	250	250	250
Wages	2000	2000	2000	2000	2000	2000	2000	2000	2000	2000	2000	2000
Telephone	50	50	50	50	50	50	50	50	50	50	50	50
Rent		300	300	300	300	300	300	300	300	300	300	300
Advertising	0	75	75	75	75	75	75					
Total payments	18200	3575	3975	4225	4225	4225	4225	4150	4150	4150	4150	4150
Closing balance	−8200	−11375	−4150	−5975	−6400	−5625	−3050	800	4650	8500	12350	14200

Unit 3 Resources

Additional resources that can be used to support student learning of this Unit are:

Textbooks

Anderton, A., *GCSE Business Studies* (Causeway Press, 2001)

Carysforth, C. and Neild, M., *BTEC First Business* (Heinemann, 2006)

Fardon, M. Nuttall, C. and Prokopiw, J., *GCSE Applied Business* (Osborne Books, 2002)

Wales, J. and Wall, N., *Nuffield–BP Business and Economics for GCSE* (2nd edn, Collins, 2001)

Websites

There are lots of websites available to help. One useful site that may provide additional information and ideas is:

www.bized.ac.uk   Bized business education site

Unit 4 Business communication

Unit overview

Unit 4 is a specialist unit for the BTEC First Certificate and BTEC First Diploma qualifications in Business. The unit gives students the chance to look in to the world of business communication including verbal and written communication.

Students are asked to consider the purpose of different types of communication in business, including the channels of communication that are available and appropriate for use in the business world, such as the use of meetings and the telephone.

Oral communication is also studied within this unit, with the purpose of allowing students to focus on their ability to listen and on how to convey themselves in both one-to-one and group working situations.

Written communication also represents a key part of the unit, with the opportunity to demonstrate skills by producing and explaining the use of different documents used within business. These documents are considered according to their layout, use and purpose, e.g. recording or reporting.

Interpersonal skills and dealing with confidentiality are the final issues to be considered and give students the opportunity to reflect on their abilities to help them with their eventual transfer in to the workplace.

Suggested activities

The table on the following page shows how activities in this Assessment and Delivery Resource cover the four different outcomes of the Unit. There are a variety of tasks including discussion material, worksheets, case studies and presentation material.

The research tasks have been prepared to allow students to gather evidence in note form to help them produce their own work.

How this unit will be assessed

To gain a Pass, learners will need to:

P1 describe, using examples, the purpose of business communications in four different business contexts

P2 respond to oral instructions conveying a series of routine business tasks

P3 make an individual contribution to a group discussion relating to business tasks and record the outcomes of the discussion

P4 produce three documents of different types to support straightforward business tasks

P5 demonstrate interpersonal and non-verbal communication skills when demonstrating business communications.

To gain a Merit requires learners to complete all the Pass requirements plus the Merit requirements, where they need to:

M1 explain how oral communications can be used in business situations

M2 give reasons for selecting appropriate documents and layouts for business purposes

M3 explain the interpersonal and non-verbal communication skills used to support effective communication.

To gain a Distinction requires a learner to complete all the Pass and Merit requirements plus the Distinction requirements, where they need to:

D1 analyse the effectiveness of oral and written communications in a given business context

D2 evaluate the importance of effective interpersonal and non-verbal communication skills in a given business context.

Learning outcomes

The unit is based on the following learning outcomes

1. Understand the purpose of communications in business contexts
2. Be able to use oral communication in business contexts
3. Be able to complete and use written business documents
4. Be able to use interpersonal and non-verbal business communication skills.

At-a-glance

Business communication 77

Activity type and description	Delivery notes	Extra resources	Links to grading criteria	Links to textbook
Outcome 1 Understand the purpose of communications in business contexts				
4.1 Introductory activity: Why communicate?	This activity asks students to think about the purpose behind different types of communication by writing the appropriate one in the box.		P1	Pages 140–143
4.2 Discussion activity: Formal or informal?	This activity asks students to consider how they could communicate informally or formally in different business situations, e.g. in a meeting or on the telephone.		P1, P4	Pages 140–143
4.3 Presentation activity: Communicating to your class	This activity asks students to produce a PowerPoint presentation or poster giving details about communication differences. Completing a mind-map at the start of the activity may stimulate further discussion.	Books or other reference materials, access to websites	P1	Pages 140–143
Outcome 2 Be able to use oral communication in business contexts				
4.4 Introductory activity: Following instructions	This activity seeks to catch out students by asking them to read the instructions and then, in instruction 10, only asking them to do one task. This activity needs a time limit linked to the ability of the group.		P2	Pages 145–146
4.5 Discussion/ role-play activity: Facing away	Another activity that considers the importance of listening and body language for clues to the communication.		P2, M1	Pages 145–148

© Harcourt Education 2006

Activity type and description	Delivery notes	Extra resources	Links to grading criteria	Links to textbook
4.6 Worksheet: Are you listening?	This listening activity gives students the chance to consider how much of the time they are actually listening, and then compare what they have heard to the message read to them.	Worksheet on CD-ROM. Paper and pens.	P2, M1	Pages 145–148
4.7 Discussion activity: Listening to a message	Two answer phone messages have been left for students to carry out two routine tasks as a result. These messages need to be recorded before the lesson based on the text supplied.	Equipment with the ability to record voice, e.g. tape recorder or laptop	P2	Pages 148–150
4.8 Worksheet: Which is best?	This activity provides a good basis for considering different methods of communication in business situations. These can then be applied to different business contexts.	Worksheet on CD-ROM	P2, M1	Pages 150–155
4.9 Discussion activity: Helping a charity	This activity asks students to take part in a discussion and then make notes about it individually. This allows students to compare how their set of notes is different from those of other people in their group. This can prompt discussion about different listening skills, the message, etc.	Pens, A4 paper	P3	Pages 151–153
4.10 Discussion activity: Judging communication!	This activity should help students work towards the D1 criteria by breaking down the stages needed to give a judgement about the appropriateness of different types of communication.		P2, M1, D1	Pages 145–155
4.11 Plenary activity: Monitoring a meeting	This activity makes use or voice or video recording equipment to allow students to hear or see themselves working in a meeting. The students are then asked to show how much time was spent discussing different parts of the meeting and the amount individuals contributed using two pie charts.	Video or voice recording equipment, coloured pens, rulers	P3	Pages 150–155

Business communication

Activity type and description	Delivery notes	Extra resources	Links to grading criteria	Links to textbook
Outcome 3 Be able to complete and use written business documents				
4.12 Introductory activity: Spot the errors!	A badly done memo that needs correcting is given for students – it has problems in terms of its layout, timing and spelling.		P4, P5	Pages 157–167
4.13 Presentation activity: In the right order?	A mixed-up letter that students need to put back together is presented here. It would be useful to put the activity on to card and then ask them to cut out and rearrange the parts.	Card, scissors	P4	Pages 159–167
4.14 Worksheet: When would you use it and why?	Different types of written communication are given and students are asked to explain when they would use each one in business and why.	Worksheet on CD-ROM, Pens	P4, M2	Pages 157–170
4.15 Case study: Brown's Electronic Gadgets	This activity is designed to help students consider the effectiveness of different types of written communication depending on the purpose of the activity. They are asked to help Brown's choose the best method to send out information or think of another type themselves based on factors such as the number of people involved, the type of product etc. The use of the internet for further research or newspaper articles on different methods of communication may be useful.	Internet	P4, M2, D1	Pages 159–167
Outcome 4 Be able to use interpersonal and non-verbal business communication skills				
4.16 Introductory activity: Self-assessment checklist	The checklist allows students to identify areas of their own interpersonal and non-verbal skills that they could be working on. This could also be used to stimulate discussion on areas such as controlling stress, asking for help etc		P5, M3	Pages 174–178

© Harcourt Education 2006

Activity type and description	Delivery notes	Extra resources	Links to grading criteria	Links to textbook
4.17 Presentation activity: Presenting yourself	By giving a presentation on tips for interpersonal and non-verbal skills students can research this area but also get valuable advice and tips by actually giving the presentation. If this is too difficult to do individually for students they could be placed on small groups to provide each other with support.	PowerPoint or handout materials, pens, paper, etc.	P5, M3, D2	Pages 174–178
4.18 PowerPoint presentation: Non-verbal communication	Using images this PowerPoint presentation gives the students a chance to consider some of the elements of non-verbal communication.		P5	Pages 174–178
4.19 Research activity: Reflecting on activity	Asking students to think about their college day and identify the activities that they do may help them to consider their use of communication – part of their interpersonal skill management. They can put their activities into three categories and consider how to decrease activities that are not useful to them.		P5, M3	Pages 174–178

Unit 4 Activities

4.1 Introductory activity: Why communicate?

Student book pages 140–143

Different types of communication have different purposes. For each of the scenarios given in the table, describe the purpose of each type of communication, choosing from the list below:

- to promote
- to confirm
- to inform
- to make a request
- to instruct

Scenario	Purpose
A national furniture company phoning a customer to say a delivery will be late	
A meeting between a supervisor and employee to receive targets to be done for that day	
A hotel ringing to let a customer know that a booking has been made and to check details	
A letter being sent to a former customer letting them know about special offers	
A family going on holiday asking for the same room they stayed in last year	
An employee going on a training course giving details to the training provider that they are vegetarian.	
An email being sent with details of a payment that has been made	
A text message being sent with a web link to a money-off voucher	

4.2 Discussion activity: Formal or informal?

Student book pages 140–143

Sometimes the way that you communicate is formal, and at other times informal.

For each example, state whether the communication is formal, informal or both:

Communication	Formal	Informal
Meetings		
Telephone		
Talking with your supervisor		
Talking with other employees		
Talking with your teacher		
Email		
Website		

4.3 Presentation activity: Communicating to your class

Student book pages 140–143

Produce a PowerPoint presentation or poster including the following detail:

1. Explain what is meant by formal and informal communication, and give examples of each type
2. Explain why keeping information to yourself is so important
3. What might happen to your organisation if the information wasn't kept secure.

4.4 Introductory activity: Following instructions

Student book pages 145–146

Make sure you read these instructions carefully and do what they say.

1. Read all instructions carefully before you begin.
2. Write your name on the top of this paper.
3. Write down the names of three different type of business document.
4. Describe the difference between formal and informal communication.
5. What is meant by email?
6. Why is dealing with customer complaints so important for a business?
7. How does body language communicate how you are feeling?
8. What might happen if you don't hear an instruction correctly?
9. What is meant by a jotter note?
10. Now you have read all the instructions, only follow the second instruction.

4.5 Discussion/role-play activity: Facing away

Student book pages 145–150

Another important part of listening and communicating verbally is actually giving eye contact and signals that the message is being heard; for example, nodding or smiling.

In pairs, without looking at the person you are working with, talk for about 1 minute about what you did at the weekend. Give no eye contact or messages to the other person at all.

1. How did this feel for the person who was telling their story?
2. How did this feel for the person listening to it?
3. How important are body language and clues when you are communicating?

4.6 Worksheet activity: Are you listening?

Student book pages 145–148

See CD-ROM

4.7 Discussion activity: Listening to a message

Student book pages 148–150

1   Read the following two answerphone messages and follow the instructions given.
2   In small groups, discuss which set of instructions was easier to follow and why this was.

Message 1

This is Mr Sykes. Please could you prepare a poster to be displayed around the college giving details about the Health Promotion Event that is to take place two weeks on Monday. You will need to clearly give details about the event which takes place between 12 and 2 in the student canteen. There will be free information and advice about all aspects of health, from weight management, smoking and exercise, to how to deal with exam stress. I would like the poster done on A4 paper and for it to be nice and bold, and to include at least one picture. Let me know if you have any problems with that.

Message 2

Please could you send an email or letter to your class teacher letting them know what you think about how you are doing on the course so far. You should include details about what you have studied in school before, why you chose this course and how much you have enjoyed the units so far. If you can think of any constructive comments about how the course could be improved that would be useful as well. Thanks, Jordan Miller.

4.8 Worksheet activity: Which is best?

Student book pages 150–155

See CD-ROM

4.9 Discussion activity: Helping a charity

Student book pages 151–153

In your class you have been divided into teams to come up with an idea to raise some money for a charity of your choice. Discuss in your team how this could happen, taking into account the following issues:

- resources
- time
- skills
- publicity
- permission from your teacher to do your activity
- health and safety.

At the end of your discussion you should each go and write notes about what you discussed. Put them on to an A4 sheet of paper that could be displayed in your classroom.

When you have all finished, compare the notes that you have all made. Were they all the same? Were they different? Why did this happen?

4.10 Discussion activity: Judging communication!

Student book pages 145–155

Analyse the advantages and disadvantages of these methods of communication in some practical situations. What is your overall judgement in each case?

Method	Reasons why this method is suitable	Reasons why this method may not be suitable	Judgement
A meeting of 20 people to discuss an advertising campaign			

4.10 Discussion activity: Judging communication! (continued)

A telephone call to tell someone their contract is not being renewed at work			
A presentation about new changes that affect the whole organisation next year			
A voicemail giving details about how to access a new website with complicated information to download for staff			
A telephone conference call giving details to three candidates about whether or not they have been successful at getting a job			
A discussion between six members of staff to talk about the bad behaviour of an employee			

4.11 Plenary activity: Monitoring a meeting

Student book pages 150–155

Have a meeting to talk about possible improvements to the way that your course could be delivered next year.

You could think about the activities, units and businesses you have studied this year.

Which ones did you think were really useful?

Which ones were good but could be made even better?

Using voice recording equipment such as a tape recorder or video camera, make an electronic record of the meeting.

Play the recording back and, using the circles a bit like pie charts, divide them up to show how much time was spent on each area of the discussion and how much time each individual person contributed. You may find it useful to have coloured pens to help you make each section clear.

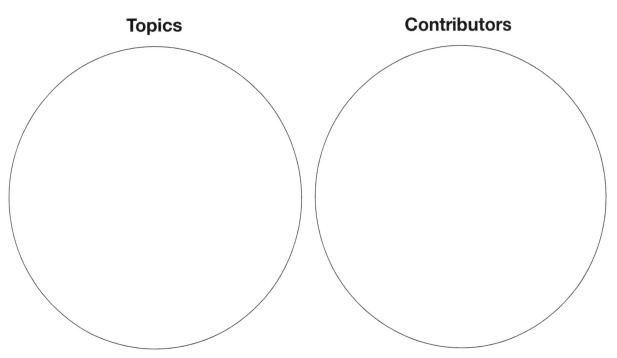

Topics   **Contributors**

1 What do you notice about your own contribution – how much time was allocated to you?
2 Were there people who spoke a lot and some who did not contribute much?
3 How could you try and make sure everyone has a fair chance to contribute?

4.12 Introductory activity: Spot the errors!

Student book pages 157–167

Here is a memo that has been sent round to staff on 20 November. There are a number of problems with it. Find the errors and then re-write the memo correctly, adding extra details that you think are needed.

> Date 18 November
>
> To Staff
>
> Memo
>
> There is a problem with car paking on our smaller site at the moement. We need to have spaces for customers so culd all staff please make sure they park round the back or try to car share if poss.
>
> All staff must also displaye a parking permit in there front window to show that they can park their. We will be cheking the cars on 20 November and any cars found without a permit will be clamped until they get their permit sorted out. This should stop people who don't work hear from parking in our spaces.

4.13 Plenary activity: In the right order?

Student book pages 159–167

Below are elements of a letter sent by E-Books Ltd to Mrs Brown, but they have got mixed up. Put them in the right order.

Element	Order
Yours sincerely	
We have a number of new titles that we are adding to our collection so I have included an information pack for you to look at. Please let me know if you would like any more information, or if you would like to place an order for any of these publications.	
Thank you for your recent order for two E-books. We are currently processing your order and hope to despatch it to you within two weeks.	
Sales Administrator	
Mrs C Brown 84 Laxford Ave Chidham LEXINGTON LE8 7PS	
J Morris	
I can be contacted by telephone on 02938 398836 or by email on jmorris@ebooksltd.co.uk	
Enc	
E-books are a new revolutionary way to read so we are sure you will enjoy reading *Black Beauty* and *Gone with the Wind* in this new electronic format.	
E Books Ltd 72 Bradshaw Close TOTHAMPTON TO72 8ZU	
Dear Mrs Brown	
19 December	

Outcome 3

4.14 Worksheet: When would you use it and why?

Student book pages 157–170

See CD-ROM

4.15 Case study: Brown's Electronic Gadgets

Student book pages 159–167

Brown's Electronic Gadgets have got a new product – voice recording pens – that they want to start selling to customers as soon as possible. These pens are easy to use and allow the user to hear previously recorded text that they can then write notes from. This means that people don't need to make as many notes when they get back to their offices, because they can hear them as they write! The company needs to get the information to 5000 people.

Joan Brown thinks that the best way to get the information to customers is by letter, as she thinks people are more likely to read it. She thinks it may be helpful to give out a money-off coupon and that they have a large number of addresses of previous customers.

Sarah Brown thinks the best way is to use email, including a video clip of how to use the product within the email. Brown's have a limited number of email addresses, but could buy a list of possible customers from an agency. This list would be available for use in one week.

Cherie Brown thinks the best way is to use a text message, using the data collected on previous customers. This could refer customers to the website for more information.

Each of these people thinks they are right!

Your task is to help them choose which method is the most likely to be effective using the criteria below. Make comments about how easy or difficult, and the advantages or disadvantages of using each method for this communication.

	Post	**Email**	**Text**
Number of people			
Type of people			
Speed of message			

4.15 Case study: Brown's Electronic Gadgets (continued)

	Post	**Email**	**Text**
Appropriate type of message			
Cost			
Image of the company			
Ease of sending			
Professional image of the business			

1 Which of these methods should they choose? Give a judgement based on their potential effectiveness.

2 What would you recommend – one of these methods or something different?

4.16 Introductory activity: Self-assessment checklist

Student book pages 174–178

Before you can explain your own interpersonal and non-verbal communication skills at work, complete this exercise to think about how you behave on a daily basis. Note any areas where you think you should do better, and then highlight them with a pen so that you can work on them.

Skill	How I behave
Being organised	
Being on time	
Being polite at all times	
Planning	
Having good personal hygiene	
Wearing clean clothes and shoes	
Keep things that I have been told confidentially to myself	
Swearing	
Chewing gum	
Interrupting others	
Arguing or shouting	
Listening	
Being friendly and welcoming, e.g. smiling	

Which three areas could I work on?

1 _____

2 _____

3 _____

4.17 Presentation activity: Presenting yourself

Student book pages 174–178

Produce a presentation, using either technology such as PowerPoint or presentation cards or handouts to help you.

This presentation should give others tips on how to present themselves better by making good use of their interpersonal and non-verbal skills.

Explain how good use of each type of skill can help you in the workplace – give a judgement about which skills you think are the most important that they should focus on.

At the end of the presentation ask some of the students in your class to give you feedback on the content of the presentation and also your skills in delivering it!

4.18 Powerpoint presentation: Non-verbal communication

Student book pages 174–178

See CD-ROM

4.19 Research activity: Reflecting on activity

Student book pages 174–178

Effective communication includes using your time effectively as well as having good interpersonal skills. For one day, write down everything that you have done during your day at college, from when you arrive to when you go home. Include everything, for example:

- Reading the *BTEC First* book
- Completing handouts with your teacher
- Researching on the Internet
- Chatting to friends
- Eating lunch
- Reading emails
- Answering emails
- Talking with your subject teacher
- Talking with your tutor
- Sending text messages
- Answering your phone
- Buying sweets, drinks. etc.

Now sort out these activities into three types:

- communications that I must do today to help me progress
- communications that I could do another day to help me progress
- communications that I didn't need to do today to help me progress.

Compare the numbers in each of these categories. How do you spend your time in a day? Do you mostly do things you must do to progress, or things you didn't need to do?

1. Which type of communication do you do most often?
2. How many different types of communication do you use?
3. Compare your results with another student in your group.
4. Think about how you can reduce the list of things you didn't need to do, so that you can spend that time working on things you do need to do.

Outcome 4

Business communication 95

Unit 4 Exemplar assignment

Assignment 4.2

Background to the assignment

This assignment is aiming to help you achieve:

P4 Produce three documents of different types to support straightforward business tasks

M2 Give reasons for selecting appropriate documents and layouts for business purposes.

You are working as an administrator for a small parcel delivery company in your area, known as FastPost Ltd.

Task 1 (P4)

See handwritten note on next page.

You have been left two tasks to do on your desk. To achieve P4, you will need to produce the documents required.

A piece of headed paper is attached for your use, including the business logo.

As part of your duties you are asked to prepare a variety of business documents to support meetings and other communication that goes on throughout the company.

Task 2 (M2)

For each of the documents you have produced you will need to explain why you chose the document that you did for that particular task and what made you make decisions about the layout, font, language, headings, etc., that you used to produce each document.

Note

To: C. Marshall

From: JBL

(a) An apology needs to be sent on official company paper to a customer who received their parcel dented. Please enclose a £5 voucher for a local shop as a gesture of good will and ask the customer to get in touch again if they need any more information. The customer's details are Mrs Sarah Smythe, The Barclays, West Torrington, WT6 7PU.

(b) Following the change in the law banning smoking in public places, FastPost have decided to make their site smoke-free. Let all staff know that from 1 August smoking will be banned from the whole site as well as in lorries or cars driven by FastPost staff. If anyone has any queries ask them to get back to Vikki Read in Human Resources. She is able to provide information on how to give up smoking. The information should go out with the subject heading of SMOKING BAN and be sent from T Race (Managing Director).

(c) There is a meeting next week of the management team. Mr Race wants it to be held in the boardroom at 3.30 p.n. on Wednesday. He has the minutes of the last meeting to go through, then matters arising and wants to have Sales Targets as the first item. Sarah Stone has asked for the employee incentive scheme to be added as an item, Bob Flemming wants to add Employee Morale and Jim Beam wants to talk about the office party. Please circulate to everyone involved.

**FastPost Ltd
Farlington Industrial Estate
Biddleham
BH7 3PQ**
Telephone 04590 892003
Fax 04590 892004
Email enquiries@fastpostltd

The Barclays
West Torrington
WT6 7PU

Dear Mrs Smyth

We are sorry to hear that you were not happy about your parcel being dented. We are sorry that this has happened. We try to make sure our drivers are careful with parcels.

We have decided to give you a £5 voucher for Woolworths as part of our apologies.

Yours sincerely

C Marshall
Administrator

Memo

To: All Staff **Date:** 26 May

From: T Race (MD) **Ref:** SB1

SMOKING BAN

Mr Race has decided that no one is going to be allowed to smoke from 1 August as part of the general ban on smoking in public places in England.

The smoking ban means that employees will not be allowed to smoke anywhere on the site including the cars and lorries when they are being driven around.

If you would like to give up smoking or have any queries about this please speak to Vikki Read in Human Resources.

Task 1

FastPost Ltd

Meeting of the Senior Management Team

3.30 pm 2 June

Agenda

1. Minutes

2. Matters Arising

3. Sales Targets

4. Employee Incentive Scheme

5. Employee Morale

6. Office Party

Assessor feedback

Task 1

You have produced the correct documents for each task so well done for identifying the correct task for the job but there are some improvements that you need to make to each document before it is fully complete.

Letter

Your letter layout needs a little work as you only used a tiny amount of the space. It may be better to use a larger or clearer font so that Mrs Smythe is able to read it more easily. It is important that Smythe is spelt correctly as this may cause her to be annoyed about the mis-spelling of her name. You also need to add a date to the letter and make sure that you put Enc to show you have included a voucher. Finally add a bit more content so she has more to read or it may not look like the business is truly sorry about the damage.

Memo

Your memo contains the basic information needed. It may be better to write the memo in the passive – this means that you write 'it has been decided to ban smoking' rather than 'Mr Race has decided'.

Agenda

It is really important on an agenda to include all the necessary details including where the meeting is to take place. The last item on the agenda will always be AOB which stands for Any Other Business. Don't forget to add your initials to the agenda so show it was prepared by you.

Task 2

You have not given an answer for Task 2 but to improve this work to work towards M2 you will need to give your reasons for why you chose the documents you did to give the information and the types of layout that you should take into account when writing business documents such as

- use of fonts
- headings
- formats
- accuracy
- fitness for what is needed.

Unit 4 Resources

Additional resources that can be used to support student learning of this Unit are:

Textbooks

Carysforth, C. and Neild, M., *BTEC First Business* (Heinemann, 2006)

Anderton, Alain, *GCSE Business Studies* (Causeway Press, 1998)

Carysforth, Carol, *Communication for Work* (Heinemann Education, 1998)

Fardon, Michael, Nuttall, Chris and Prokopiw, John, *GCSE Applied Business* (Osborne Books, 2002)

Miles, P., *Business and Communication Systems GCSE* (Nelson Thornes, 2003)

Websites

There are lots of websites available to help. One useful site that may provide additional information and ideas is:

www.bized.ac.uk   Bized business education site

Unit 5 People in organisations

Unit overview

Unit 5 is a specialist unit for the BTEC First Certificate and BTEC First Diploma qualifications in Business. The unit aims to help students understand the wide range of people, roles and responsibilities within the workplace.

The unit seeks to prepare students for the workplace by encouraging them to reflect on their own skills and abilities before matching those to suitable types of employment. During the unit they will investigate the relationships between managers and employees and the importance of those relationships in order to build better businesses.

The unit emphasises the importance of the different roles needed to make a business effective and the skills that are needed within those roles. The need to be flexible, adaptable and to provide skills as individuals and as an organisation as a whole is studied.

The unit starts with students reflecting on their own skills, knowledge, qualifications and interests in choosing a job. Students then go on to consider terms and conditions of employment including the relevant legislation that influences the working environment. Different types of organisational structures and team working are examined before the final aspect of the unit requires students to consider the review process within the workplace on a formal and informal basis as well as the need for clear career development planning. By completing this unit students should be able to gain a good understanding of the workplace that will help them to find work or work experience effectively.

Suggested activities

The table on the following pages shows how activities in this Assessment and Delivery Resource cover the four different outcomes of the Unit. There are a variety of tasks including discussion material, worksheets, case studies and presentation material.

The research tasks have been prepared to allow students to gather evidence in note form to help them produce their own work.

How this unit will be assessed

To gain a Pass, learners will need to:

P1 match current knowledge and skills to possible job opportunities using appropriate sources of information and advice

P2 complete an application for a selected job opportunity

P3 describe the terms and conditions of employment in a selected organisation

P4 describe how working practices are developed

P5 produce a career development plan using performance reviews.

To gain a Merit requires learners to complete all the Pass requirements plus the Merit requirements, where they need to:

M1 explain the importance of terms and conditions of employment

M2 compare and contrast the organisational structures and job roles within two business organisations

M3 explain the importance of team working and personal attributes within two business organisations.

To gain a Distinction requires a learner to complete all the Pass and Merit requirements plus the Distinction requirements, where they need to:

D1 analyse, using examples, the implications of terms and conditions of employment

D2 evaluate how personal attributes and team working contribute to working practices.

Learning outcomes

The unit is based on the following learning outcomes

1. Know how to prepare for employment
2. Understand terms and conditions of employment
3. Know how working practices are developed
4. Be able to plan career development.

© Harcourt Education 2006

At-a-glance

Activity type and description	Delivery notes	Extra resources	Links to grading criteria	Links to textbook
Outcome 1 Know how to prepare for employment				
5.1 Introductory activity: Skills gap mind-map	This mind-map helps students to think about possible ideas for employment that they would like in the future and the type of experience and knowledge that students would need to do those jobs. Measuring the skills gap can help students to make reasoned choices about what they should do next in terms of work experience or study.	Pens, paper, whiteboard	P1	Pages 182–185
5.2 Case study: Pontin's	This case study looks at the type of training offered to permanent and casual staff at Pontin's as well as the skills and knowledge needed by those staff. Students are asked to consider the differences between employees and the benefits and limitations of training seasonal employees.	Pens and paper, PC with access to Pontin's website if required	P1	Pages 184–185
5.3 Worksheet: Skills questionnaire	This skills questionnaire asks students to identify what they are good at via the option 'very like me' and show which areas they need to work on – 'not like me'. By ranking them in order of the importance to the student, the student is able to construct a form of action plan to help them work on these skills areas.	Worksheet on CD-ROM. Pens	P1	Pages 182–185
5.4 Research activity: North Lincolnshire Council online applications	This activity shows students how online applications work – this can be a useful task to work on as a demonstration in class with everyone making notes or as an individual activity. By considering the benefits and issues that students may feel about applying online they can start to appreciate the problems they may encounter when applying in this way.		P2	Pages 187–192
5.5 Worksheet: Match the terms	A quick way for students to reinforce their understanding of common terms such as temporary or permanent by matching them to their meanings.	Worksheet on CD-ROM	P1	Pages 182–192

Activity type and description	Delivery notes	Extra resources	Links to grading criteria	Links to textbook
5.6 Worksheet: Browns Ltd	This activity asks students to write a letter of application. It will be useful for them to referred to the student book for Unit 5 so that they can be reminded of the key points that should be present within a letter of application.	Worksheet on CD-ROM. Access to a PC.	P2	Pages 192, 196
5.7 Worksheet: Which candidate would you choose?	This is a follow-on activity from 5.6 and asks students to consider two letters of application that have been sent in, and to choose which one they would interview. Both have weaknesses, so students are asked how they could be improved.	Worksheet on CD-ROM	P2	Pages 187–192
5.8 Plenary activity: A Business Studies teacher	A chance for students to consider the skills and knowledge required by their own teacher – what training have they received, which qualifications do they have, and so on.		P1	Page 189
Outcome 2 Understand terms and conditions of employment				
5.9 Introductory activity: Contr8ct	This ready made mind-map gives students the chance to think about the 8 pieces of information that must be contained within a contract of employment. This activity may be used as a way to get students to think about what should be there or could be used as research when combined with the BTEC First Business text book.	Pens	P3	Pages 197–198
5.10 Worksheet: Statutory?	This activity asks students to categorise whether or not certain rights within a contract are statutory or contractual. The BTEC First Business text book will provide help for this task.	Worksheet on CD-ROM. Pens	P3	Pages 197–202
5.11 Worksheet: Must have, can be given, access to?	Again, looking at contractual rights, this activity asks students to consider what information must be contained within the contract, what can be given and what sort of information employees should be given access to.	Worksheet on CD-ROM. Pens	P3	Pages 197–202
5.12 Discussion activity: Probation	This discussion asks students to think about how long probation should last. Discussing the importance of terms and conditions, such as probationary period, would fulfil the M1 criterion.		P1, M1	Page 198

Activity type and description	Delivery notes	Extra resources	Links to grading criteria	Links to textbook
5.13 Discussion activity: Reputation	This discussion asks students to think about the smoking bans given to employees by Marks and Spencer and BT to explain how policies can affect terms and conditions and the implications of this.		M1, D1	Pages 201–202, 214
5.14 PowerPoint presentation: Employment law	This PowerPoint presentation goes through the main pieces of relevant legislation and may be given as a handout to help students consider the terms and conditions of employment		P1, M1, D1	Pages 203–206, 373–379
Outcome 3 Know how working practices are developed				
5.15 Introductory activity: Different structures	Passage for students to complete with words provided. An extension strategy for this exercise is to ask students to draw the relevant organisational structures to go with it.	Pen	P4, M2	Pages 210–213
5.16 Case study: Bacardi Martini	This case study looks at the way policies affect what employees are allowed to do at work.		P3, P4, D1	Page 214
5.17 Research activity: Policies that affect you	Students are encouraged to consider how policies on behaviour, homework, smoking affect their every day conduct.			Page 214
5.18 Worksheet: Job roles	Students are asked to match the activities presented to the correct level of job role – senior manager, middle manager and junior manager.	Worksheet on CD-ROM	P4, M2	Pages 215–217
5.19 Presentation activity: Presenting yourself	Students are given the task of producing a 1-minute presentation on what they think is important in terms of personal presentation – revision of Unit 2 and practical help with ideas for assignment work.		M2	Pages 219–220
5.20 Discussion/role-play: Real challenge	This team-based activity asks students to work in teams and then reflect on how they did.	Card, pens, scissors, glue, etc.	M3, D2	Pages 217–219

People in organisations 107

Activity type and description	Delivery notes	Extra resources	Links to grading criteria	Links to textbook
Outcome 4 Be able to plan career development				
5.21 Introductory activity: When have you had your performance reviewed?	Students are given the chance to think about the number of times their performance has been reviewed in their life as part of their own development and then their career development.. This is an opportunity to review how they felt about this process	Pens	P5	Pages 223–225
5.22 Discussion activity: Performance	This discussion asks students to consider whether pay should be linked to performance and the benefits (e.g. productivity and motivation) or problems (e.g. fairness), relationships between manager and employee, competition between employees, and expectation of receiving motivation/de-motivation. Opportunity here to discuss with students their performance monitoring in work.		P5	Pages 223–225
5.23 Role-play activity: The review process	This role play allows students to experience giving feedback, receiving it and watching the process. It gives an opportunity for constructive comments to be made to students about how to improve.		P5	Pages 223–225
5.24 Worksheet: Time-line	This worksheet allows students to think about their short- and long-term career planning. This activity could be used as part of notes/information to write up for P5. The activity also considers what might limit progress, and could provide an opportunity to think of ways around this.	Worksheet on CD-ROM	P5	Pages 225–227

© Harcourt Education 2006

Activity type and description	Delivery notes	Extra resources	Links to grading criteria	Links to textbook
5.25 Presentation: Careers advisor	This activity asks students to give a presentation or make a display giving advice on careers in business and in particular two or three jobs that the student may be planning to do in future. This activity can be extended by asking for more details or reduced by asking for details about only one type of job.	PowerPoint presentation cards. Materials for a display, e.g. card, glue, paper, pens, photos, etc. Access to careers materials or websites	P5	Pages 225–227

Unit 5 Activities

5.1 Introductory activity: Skills gap mind-map

Student book pages 182–185

Think of as many jobs as you can that you would like to do in the future, and write them down on a piece of paper as a mind-map.

Extend each job by adding any special skills or experience you need to do them.

Do you have any relevant experience yet?

Now measure the gap between what you already have and what you need.

This is known as the skills gap, and you will need to be aware of this gap to plan how you can achieve as much as you want to.

5.2 Case study: Pontin's

Student book pages 184–185

Some businesses take employees on all year round, and these are called permanent employees. Others take people on only for a season or short length of time during a year – these are known as seasonal or temporary workers.

Pontin's Holiday Centres employ over 300 permanent staff and 1600 seasonal staff to cope with the 600,000 customers who visit them each year. To encourage seasonal employees to return to the organisation each year, Pontin's spend lots of money training staff. They give each member of staff:

- a personal development file with job descriptions and aims
- access to NVQs
- access to vocational training funding to study qualifications such as BTEC First Business
- help with professional qualifications
- an assessment of aims and goals, and help in achieving them.

By investing in their staff in this way and helping them to improve their skills to match to the jobs that they do, Pontin's have more staff returning to them and fewer staff leaving.

1. What is the difference between seasonal and permanent employees?
2. Who might help an employee fill in their personal development file?
3. Which kind of skills do you think you might need to work at a holiday camp like Pontin's?

5.3 Worksheet: Skills questionnaire

Student book pages 182–185

See CD-ROM

5.4 Research activity: North Lincolnshire Council online applications

Student book pages 187–192

Many businesses ask you to make an application online for a job. This means that you may only have one chance to complete your answers on-screen, and this means you need to think quickly and carefully to avoid mistakes. North Lincolnshire Council use an online application form, which you can find by accessing their website www.northlincs.gov.uk, and going to the section 'jobs and careers' followed by the online application form.

1   What do you think is good about doing an online application?
2   What might the problems be?

5.5 Worksheet: Match the terms

Student book pages 182–192

See CD-ROM

5.6 Worksheet: Browns Ltd

Student book pages 192, 196

See CD-ROM

5.7 Worksheet: Which candidate would you choose?

Student book pages 187–192

See CD-ROM

5.8 Plenary activity: A Business Studies teacher

Student book page 189

1   Make a list of the skills and knowledge that you would need to become the ideal Business Studies teacher.

2   How do teachers apply to be teachers and what do they need to do to work in your college or school?

Outcome 1

5.9 Introductory activity: Contr8ct

Student book pages 197–198

Which eight pieces of information must be contained within a contract of employment?

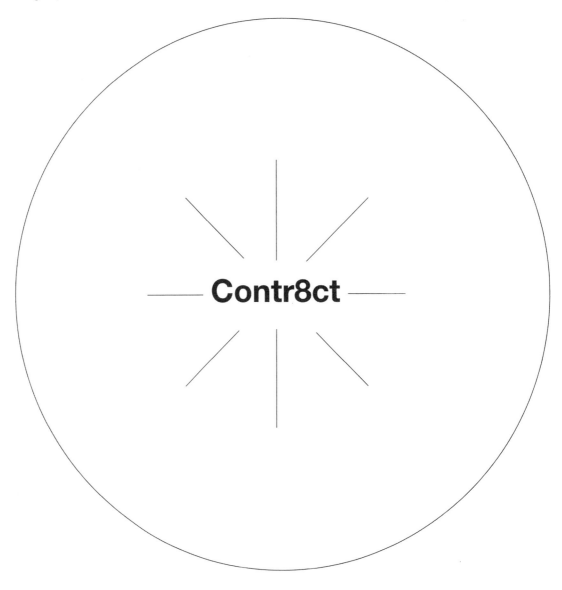

5.10 Worksheet: Statutory?

Student book pages 197–202

See CD-ROM

People in organisations 113

5.11 Worksheet: Must have, can be given, access to?

**Student book
pages 197–202**

See CD-ROM

5.12 Discussion activity: Probation

**Student book
page 198**

Probation is the amount of time an employee works on a job before they are officially taken on by the organisation. This is time when they prove they are suitable for the job.

Discuss as a class or in small groups how long you think someone should be on probation for: 3 months, 6 months or a year?

5.13 Discussion activity: Reputation

**Student book
pages 201–202, 214**

Recently there have been several cases where employees have been told they can or cannot do things while working for an employer. Marks and Spencer told employees in April 2006 not to smoke while in their uniforms in case they damage the company's reputation, and BT told their employees in March 2006 not to smoke on company premises or inside company vans. As these are policies held by each organisation, they become terms and conditions of employment to work there. Discuss the importance of terms and conditions of employment and the implications for employees of these changes in policy.

5.14 PowerPoint presentation: Employment law

**Student book
pages 203–206, 373–379**

See CD-ROM

Outcome 2

© Harcourt Education 2006

5.15 Introductory activity: Different structures

Student book pages 210–213

Fill in the gaps, using the words from the list on the next page.

An organisational structure shows, in diagram form, the way that jobs are organised. It shows very clearly who _____ which employees.

There are three main types of structure that are used within organisations. These are the **hierarchical**, _____ and **matrix** structures. Hierarchical structures are those which have many _____ and look like a _____ in shape.

Flat structures have _____ layers between the most senior person in the _____ to the employees at the _____ of the structure, so they look flat.

Matrix structures cross over _____ between different _____ , so that teams are formed on projects from all areas of the business, for example the Finance Manager, Human Resources Manager and the _____ Manager all working on Project 1.

The **hierarchical** structure is the most _____ structure, which some people call a pyramid structure. This is because it looks like a pyramid. There are fewer people at the top of the structure, who manage people below them. At the lower levels there are more employees and fewer managers. **Flat** structures have fewer management levels, so managers are often _____ for more people compared to a hierarchical organisation.

By having fewer layers of _____ in the organisation, _____ tends to flow more quickly from the top to the bottom. This can make decision-making or problem-solving quicker, as _____ people are involved in making a _____ , and fewer managers need to be _____.

The final type of organisation is that of the **matrix** structure. This structure has links between departments that start to look like a spider's _____. This type of structure makes _____ in the organisation from each of the departments. This means that team working across all a _____ can happen. This type of structure is most _____ in organisations where project work is needed, because the team members are taken from all areas of the business and can provide _____ and comments from their own area of the business. This should mean that the project is more likely to be successful, as _____ will be found earlier and can be sorted out more quickly.

5.15 Introductory activity: Different structures (continued)

areas	decision	layers	marketing	projects	teams
bottom	departments	less	organisation	pyramid	traditional
common	few	management	paid	responsible	web
communication	flat	manages	problems	suggestions	

5.16 Case study: Bacardi Martini

Student book page 214

Bacardi Martini in Southampton is one of the most successful businesses in the Southampton area, and in 2006 was voted 15th in the top 100 best companies to work for. They produce and/or distribute a number of different alcoholic drinks throughout the UK and abroad.

At their factory in Southampton they have a strict policy of no drinking – this is known as a 'dry site', so employees are not allowed to consume alcohol before or during the time they are at work on the site. Bacardi also promote responsible drinking by encouraging people to enjoy a drink but not to drink to excess or binge-drink.

1. Why do you think Bacardi has the policy of not allowing drinking on its factory premises?
2. What influence might this have on working practices and the terms and conditions of employment for Bacardi employees?
3. Why are clear policies like this important in business?

5.17 Research activity: Policies that affect you

Student book page 214

Look up the policies that affect you either in your part-time job, work experience or at college/school.

1. How do these policies affect your working/studying life?
2. What are the consequences if you do not follow them?
3. How does having such policies help everyone to know what is expected of them?

5.18 Worksheet: Job roles

Student book pages 215–217

See CD-ROM

5.19 Presentation activity: Presenting yourself

Student book pages 219–220

Give a 1-minute presentation, making use of PowerPoint if you want to, on the main things that you should take into account when presenting yourself at work. Use the list below to help you with ideas.

- Personal presentation
- Verbal communication
- Written communication
- Being on time and being able to time your presentation
- Following instructions
- Being polite
- Being honest
- Being confidential.

1. Which do you think are the most important?
2. What happens if you don't present yourself in the right way?

5.20 Discussion/role-play activity: Real challenge

Student book pages 217–219

Working in a team has lots of influence over how a business works. Complete this team working activity and describe the advantages and disadvantages of working in a team.

Within your class, divide yourselves into groups of a minimum of three people. Your challenge in those groups is to come up with a design for a new type of breakfast cereal. You can use whichever ingredients your group decide, and as a group you will need to hand in a box design and a recommendation for the name and selling price of the cereal. Your teacher will give you the materials and time to do this.

At the end of the task, write in the boxes below the advantages and disadvantages of working in a team. Then add performance evaluations:

- How well do you think you performed?
- How well did the other team members think you performed?

Advantages	**Disadvantages**

What I thought of my performance	**What others thought of my performance**

Give a judgement about how important you think your own personal attributes (e.g. verbal skills, presentation, written skills, punctuality, courtesy, honesty, time planning) and team working skills were when working on this task.

5.21 Introductory activity: When have you had your performance reviewed?

Student book pages 223–225

When and how has your performance been reviewed? Fill in the boxes below.

When	How
As a baby or young child	
At school	
At college	
At outside activities, e.g. gym, membership of clubs or societies	
At your part-time job or work experience	

Consider how you felt at each of these performance reviews:

1. How much were you in control?
2. How much did you agree targets for what you could or should do?
3. How did you feel about each review?

5.22 Discussion activity: Performance

Student book pages 223–225

Some performance reviews are linked to pay. This means if you do well you may receive an increase in your rate per hour, a bonus during the year, or time off – e.g. extra holiday or being able to go home early.

Discuss how you think this might help increase the amount of work done by employees.

What might the possible problems be of linking the review to rewards such as pay for the employee, for the manager or for the organisation as a whole?

People in organisations 119

5.23 Role-play: The review process

**Student book
pages 223–225**

Get into groups of three to role-play the scenarios below. One of you is to be the manager, one the employee and one the observer. Choose one of the scenarios and role-play the employee review process. The role of the observer is to give feedback to both the manager and the employee about how they did and what they could do better. For the next scenario, change who is the manager, employee and observer until everyone has had a chance to take part in all of the roles.

Appraisal Document for Employee A

Employee A works as a sales assistant in a large chain of chemists. A has been exceeding all targets given to them by the company and is on target to get a pay rise of 20 pence per hour. They are always on time and work extremely hard. They recently received an 'Employee of the Month' award for giving really good service to a customer, and won £50. The appraisal interview is designed to congratulate A and ask them about further targets to set as part of career planning such as training.

Appraisal Document for Employee B

Employee B is working as a cook in a restaurant. B has been working well but has been regularly late in the mornings. This is because B is a single parent and has to drop their child off at school on the way in. B works extremely hard when they are at work, often working through lunch to make up extra time. B has taken many days off sick, and also parental leave to look after the child when she was sick.

Appraisal Document for Employee C

Employee C works as a receptionist in a leisure centre. C already has a written warning on file for speaking to a customer rudely. C is often late, has frequent cigarette breaks and usually has more than the specified hour for lunch. C has been counselled before about their problems and things improved for about a week and then went back to normal.

5.24 Worksheet: Time-line

**Student book
pages 225–227**

See CD-ROM

5.25 Presentation activity: Careers advisor

Student book pages 225–227

Instead of being the person getting advice, you are now going to change and become the careers advisor! Using books, information packs or websites give advice to a person who wants a career in business.

- Describe the skills they would find useful.
- Which qualifications would they need?
- What advice would you give them about Business and Business Studies courses?
- Which type of careers are there available in business? Choose two or three that you think are really good.
    - What is the pay like?
    - What are the hours like?
    - What are the chances for promotion like?

Produce a wall display of the information that can be placed in your classroom or give the advice by giving a presentation to other members of your class. Ask your teacher to help you choose which option is best for you.

People in organisations 121

Unit 5 Exemplar assignment

Assignment 5.1

Background to the assignment

For this assignment you are going to be applying for a job in business to show that you can

P1 Match current knowledge and skills to possible job opportunities using appropriate sources of information and advice.

P2 Complete an application form for a selected job opportunity.

Task 1 (P1)

Personal Skills Audit

a Using a template that you can find in Microsoft Word, or using research from the Internet and the BTEC First Business textbook, produce your own up to date Curriculum Vitae (CV). You may have a copy of a CV from school that needs to be changed and updated.

b Using your CV, complete the Skills Audit on the following page to help you identify what you are good at and the types of jobs that may be suitable for you.

c When you have completed the Skills Audit, look up three jobs that match the skills that you have identified using websites such as www.fish4jobs.co.uk or local and national newspapers. Write a paragraph on each of these jobs showing why they are suitable for you.

Task 2 (P2)

Application Form

As a student of Business Studies you have been asked to apply for the job of Office Assistant at Speedy Motors.

You are provided with the job description, person specification and application form. Using the information you collected from the skills audit and your CV, complete the application form in as much detail as possible.

Skills Audit

Fill in the skills audit below to help you identify the skills that you do well that relate to working in business, and those that you need to work on to improve them. Use a scale of 1 to 5 to measure how good you are at a particular skill:

- 1 means really weak at this skill
- 5 means really good at this skill.

You will need to measure yourself somewhere along that scale.

Skill	Rating	Skill	Rating
IT		**Communication**	
• able to use word processing		• producing business documents	
• able to use spreadsheets		• using the telephone	
• able to use databases		• filling in paperwork or forms	
• able to use email and the Internet		• giving presentations to other people in your team or workplace	
Number skills		**Team working**	
• confident in doing calculations		• working with others	
• confident to deal with cash or credit card transactions		• being a member of a social club or team	
• able to spot errors		• producing group work	
• confident to use a calculator		**Learning and training**	
Business knowledge		• able to take part in more training and learning	
• understanding of how business works		• able to ask questions and check understanding	
• understanding of what is meant by a customer and customer service		**Working under pressure**	
		• able to deal with difficult customers	
• understanding of different functions of business, e.g. human resources		• able to work under pressure	
		• able to use relaxation techniques to help cope with stress	

Task 2 documents

Speedy Motors Ltd

Job description for the position of Office Assistant

Job title	Office assistant
Department	Sales and Accounts
Responsible to	Bob Fleming
Scope of the post	Office Assistant to the Sales and Accounts team
Responsibilities	The post holder is expected to help with company accounts using Sage Accounting Software by inputting data in to the computer accurately and spotting errors. They are also responsible for • general office duties such as travel claim processing • dealing with the incoming and outgoing mail • typing letters and filing • any other duties as commensurate with the post
Compiled by	J George
Date	17 June

Person specification for the position of Office Assistant

Post title: Office assistant

Criterion	Essential	Desirable
Qualifications/knowledge:	BTEC First Business plus two other GCSEs IT skills, particularly spreadsheets and database	Ability to type quickly or touch type
Work-related experience:	No previous experience necessary but must have an understanding of how a business works	Previous experience or willingness to work in an open-plan environment
Skills/abilities and special attributes	Well organised Able to prioritise workloads Good communication skills Team-working ability Administration skills, e.g. filing and distributing the mail	Ability to use Sage accounting software

Application form
Personal details
Name Address   Telephone number Email Date of birth
Education

Dates	School or College	Qualifications	Results, predicted or actual

Work Experience or Voluntary Work		
Dates	School or College	Details

Personal interests or hobbies

Reasons for applying, specific skills related to the job and any other relevant information

References

Name	Name
Position	Position
Address	Address
Telephone	Telephone

Statement

I declare that this application form has been filled out correctly and I realise that, if I write anything that is not true, any possible job offer that I may accept may be withdrawn.

Signed   Date

Task 1a

Curriculum Vitae

Personal Details

Name	Saeed Hussain
Address	72 Lackford Ave
	Southampton
	SO14 APJ
Telephone	023 8082346
Date of Birth	2.2.89

Education

2006 - 2007	Any College
2005 - 2006	Any School

Academic Qualifications

BTEC First Business	Pass Awarded

My course covered units including

- Exploring Business Purposes
- Developing Customer Relations
- Investigating Financial Control
- People in Organisations
- Personal Selling
- Doing business online

Maths GCSE	D Grade
English GCSE	C Grade
Science GCSE	DD

Personal Statement

I really enjoy going out with my friends at the weekends. I am very interested in IT and have spent a lot of time surfing the Internet and emailing people from all over the world. My ambition one day is to run my own business selling computers or IT services.

Reference

Josh Gibbons

12 Newtown Road

Southampton

SO13 7PU

Task 1b

Saeed Hussain

Task 1b

Skills audit

Skill	Rating
IT	
• able to use word processing	3
• able to use spreadsheets	3
• able to use databases	3
• able to use email and the Internet	3
Number skills	
• confident in doing calculations	4
• confident to deal with cash or credit card transactions	4
• able to spot errors	4
• confident to use a calculator	5
Business knowledge	
• understanding of how business works	3
• understanding of what is meant by a customer and customer service	3
• understanding of different functions of business, e.g. human resources	3

Skill	Rating
Communication	
• producing business documents	3
• using the telephone	1
• filling in paperwork or forms	2
• giving presentations to other people in your team or workplace	2
Team working	
• working with others	2
• being a member of a social club or team	2
• producing group work	2
Learning and training	
• able to take part in more training and learning	5
• able to ask questions and check understanding	5
Working under pressure	
• able to deal with difficult customers	1
• able to work under pressure	1
• able to use relaxation techniques to help cope with stress	1

By looking at my skills audit I can see that I am best with figures and with computers. I like doing training to do new jobs so I would be good in a job with training. My BTEC has helped me to understand how a business works.

I don't like being under pressure or using the phone too much in a job. I am not confident at using the phone. I also don't like dealing with difficult customers or a job where I am under a lot of pressure.

I have found 3 jobs that would suit my skills from www.fish4jobs.co.uk

Task 1c

Job 1

Administration Officers

Reference ****

Job Description

We are looking for three excellent applicants to work within a busy intelligence team in Portsmouth. You must be reliable, hard working and have lots of drive and determination.

You will be working in a lively and dedicated team, attention to detail, accuracy and a willingness to take on additional duties to assist the team are imperative. You must also have the drive and determination to follow ongoing projects through from start to completion, always ensuring information is up to date, available and accurate.

This is initially a long-term temporary booking. However, there is the distinct possibility that this booking will go permanent. This is an excellent opportunity for applicants interested in working within the public sector!!!!

Please note for this booking you must be available for a minimum of 6 months

Salary	Start date	Type
£6.00 per hour	05 Jun	Temporary Position

Source: www.brookstreet.co.uk/

This job would be good for me because I am very hard working and I am good at working in a team. I have finished my course and I am looking for a full-time permanent job but I am happy to do a temporary job especially if it is for 6 months and they might decide to keep me on. I like doing project work and I am good at doing administration. The public sector means that I will be working for someone like the government or a hospital. This would be a good place to work. It says in the job description that you need to be accurate and I am good at spotting errors so this should help me.

Job 2

Task 1c

Vacancy: Administration Support - Henley-On-Thames

Web Ref:

Location: Henley

Salary: £15,000 + extensive benefits package

Job type: Permanent full-time

Division: Consulting

Purpose: We are currently seeking an administrator to fulfill a very varied support role, within the HR Solutions division of Aon, a leading pension, benefits and HR consulting firm.

Working in our recently refurbished Henley on Thames office, you will provide support across all areas, including client projects, marketing and office administration.

In terms of experience, you will need to have at least 18 months office/admin experience.

You will also need to have an excellent telephone manner and communication skills, and the willingness to get involved and work in a team.

Experience of using Microsoft Software and the internet will also be required.

Key Accountabilities: Key responsibilities will include:

- production and collation of course materials
- organising travel and accommodation arrangements
- maintaining stock levels of all office stationery
- updating various databases
- support in organising marketing events, including mailshots, research into venues, etc
- support in maintaining a tidy, client-receiving office environment

Technical knowledge requirements: In terms of experience, you will need to have at least 18 months office/admin experience.

You will also need to have an excellent telephone manner and communication skills, and the willingness to get involved and work in a team.

Experience of using Microsoft Software and the internet will also be required

Source: www.amris.com/

I would really like this job and I have lots of the skills that it asks for. I am able to use software and the internet so I would be good at this. There are some things about this job that would not suit me because I do not like dealing with the customers on the phone at all. This is something I need to improve but I like working in a team. I also don't have 18 months experience so it is not likely they will interview me so I won't apply for this job.

Task 1c

Job 3

Date: Tuesday 30th May

An established City based IT recruitment company requires an Office Administrator to support a team of Recruitment Consultants. Responsibilities include handling telephone enquiries, assisting in resourcing of clients and candidates, liaising with candidates and clients, arranging interviews, updating client/candidate database and general office administration. You must be computer-literate (MS Outlook, Word, Excel, PowerPoint) and enjoy working in a busy sales environment.

Salary: circa £20,000 p.a. (negotiable according to experience)

Location: London (City) Posting ref

Source: www.gumtree.co.uk/

I think this job would be really good for me because I really like IT and I am able to use the computer well. This is one of the things I am best at. I can use Outlook, Word, Excel and Powerpoint. I like being busy and working in a team so this job sounds good for me. I would be good at using databases so I would happy to update the database. The only difficult with this job for me might be that I do find working on the telephone more difficult and this is important so this might be difficult for me. I may be able to get more practice at this skill because it seems that lots of employers want this. This job may be good for me but I will have to be sure so I would need to talk to them a bit more about the job.

Of the 3 jobs that I have looked at, the one that seems best for me is the one in Portsmouth because it has less work with customers on the telephone than the other two.

Task 2

Task 2

Application form	
Personal details	
Name	Saeed Hussain
Address	72 Lackford Ave Southampton SO14 APJ
Telephone number	023 8082346
Email	saeedhussain@hotmail.com
Date of birth	2.2.89

Education

Dates	School or College	Qualifications	Results, predicted or actual
2006-2007	Any College	BTEC First Business	Pass
2005-2006	Any School	Maths GCSE English GCSE Science	D C DD

Work Experience or Voluntary Work

Dates	School or College	Details

Personal interests or hobbies

I really enjoy going out with my friends at the weekends. I am very interested in IT and have spent a lot of time surfing the Internet and emailing people from all over the world. My ambition one day is to run my own business selling computers or IT services.

Reasons for applying, specific skills related to the job and any other relevant information

I would really like to work as an Office Assistant because I have a real interest in computers and think I would be good at using them. I am good at filing as well and I have learned a lot about business by doing my course. We had to units on doing business online, financial control and providing business and administration support.

References

Name	Josh Gibbons	Name	
Position		Position	
Address	12 Newtown Road Southampton SO13 7PU	Address	
Telephone		Telephone	

Statement

I declare that this application form has been filled out correctly and I realise that, if I write anything that is not true, any possible job offer that I may accept may be withdrawn.

Signed *S Hussain*   Date 20 June

Exemplar assignment

Assessor feedback

Saeed you have produced some really good work for P1 by clearly matching your skills to the jobs that you found on the Internet. You have written the source of where you got the jobs from and that is really good too. Your CV also helps you to clearly see which skills and qualifications you have. One addition you could add to that is to put an extra section that is called Work Experience or Voluntary Work as many employers like to see if you have done any kind of work and I know you have been working at weekends with your uncle.

You have used the skills audit that you produced to also look at a job that does not match all of your skills so this shows that you are really thinking about what jobs would be good for you and you realise that there are some areas that you need to get more training or help with, for example using the telephone. Well done. P1 awarded.

For P2 you have completed the application form but there are some key areas missing. Your sections on reasons for applying for the job and your hobbies are really too short. This is the chance you have to let an employer know how good you really are, so please add extra detail here. Think of all the things that are really positive about you, such as the fact that you are hard-working and are always on time, etc. For P2 to be awarded, you also need to add work experience from school or from working with your uncle into the form to finish it off.

Unit 5 Resources

Additional resources that can be used to support student learning of this Unit are:

Textbooks

Carysforth, C. and Neild, M., *BTEC First Business* (Heinemann, 2006)

Martin, M. and Jackson, T., *Personnel Practice (People and Organisations)* (Chartered Institute of Personnel and Development, 2002)

Dransfield, R. *et al.*, *BTEC National Business: Student Book* (Heinemann, 2004). This resource may be useful for those students operating at Distinction level who require additional information to help them.

Websites

There are lots of websites available to help in the preparation for work area. Some useful sites that may provide additional information and ideas include:

www.bized.ac.uk	Bized business education site
www.hse.gov.uk	Health and Safety Executive website
www.investorsinpeople.co.uk	Investors in People
www.cipd.co.uk	Chartered Institute of Personnel and Development
www.businesslink.gov.uk	Support on all aspects of business including training and development
www.bbctraining.com	Free line resources to consider as part of online training
www.trainingmag.com	Training resource and news site
www.dti.gov.uk/training_development	Government supported training and development resources
www.skillbasetraining.co.uk	Training supplier
www.personneltoday.com	Provides information on training and personnel issues
www.trainingzone.co.uk	Articles, news and features to do with training

Unit 6 Providing business and administration support

Unit overview

Unit 6 is a specialist unit for the BTEC First Certificate and BTEC First Diploma qualifications in Business. The unit gives students the chance to look in to the world of business administration and support including the use of office machinery and documents needed for meetings.

Students are asked to consider the purpose of different types of support including producing documents, arranging travel, working with diaries and processing expense claims. These are skills that can usefully be transferred into the workplace via work experience or a part time job. Students will learn to be able to compare the use of electronic diaries with traditional paper-based methods.

Students are asked to consider the use of equipment for administrative and business support including the practical use of that equipment, advantages and disadvantages of the equipment and the importance of instruction manuals to help them.

Lastly students will develop skills in the process, retrieving and archiving of information to help store data and be aware of associated issues relating to the storage of information such as the need to maintain confidentiality.

Suggested activities

The table on the following page shows how activities in this Assessment and Delivery Resource cover the four different outcomes of the Unit. There are a variety of tasks including discussion material, worksheets, case studies and presentation material.

The research tasks have been prepared to allow students to gather evidence in note form to help them produce their own work.

How this unit will be assessed

To gain a Pass, learners will need to:

P1 describe the purpose and types of business and administration support

P2 operate a diary system to support business purposes

P3 demonstrate appropriate telephone techniques using the features of a telephone system

P4 describe the use of office equipment to meet different business requirements

P5 organise a meeting and provide administrative support

P6 describe the procedures needed to process, retrieve and archive information.

To gain a Merit requires learners to complete all the Pass requirements plus the Merit requirements, where they need to:

M1 compare and contrast paper and electronic diary systems

M2 explain the appropriate use of office equipment types, features and functions to suit different business purposes

M3 explain the organisation and administrative support provided for meetings.

To gain a Distinction requires a learner to complete all the Pass and Merit requirements plus the Distinction requirement, where they need to:

D1 analyse the contribution that office systems and equipment make to the provision of business and administration support

D2 analyse the organisation and administrative support provided for a meeting and recommend any improvements that could have been made.

Learning outcomes

The unit is based on the following learning outcomes

1. Understand the purpose of providing business and administration support
2. Know how to operate office systems and equipment
3. Be able to organise and provide administrative support for meetings
4. Be able to demonstrate the procedures needed to process, retrieve and archive information.

© Harcourt Education 2006

At-a-glance

Activity type and description	Delivery notes	Extra resources	Links to grading criteria	Links to textbook
Outcome 1 Understand the purpose of providing business and administration support				
6.1 Introductory activity: What do the words mean?	This activity asks students to break down what the actual phrases used for administration mean, e.g. consistency and effective – this could be used as a starter activity.		P1	Pages 232–234
6.2 Research activity: Practical activities	These activities give students the chance to practise their business administration skills by sending an email, writing a letter and researching a trip. Additional requirements could be made to add differentiation.	Internet and computer access	P1	Pages 232–234
6.3 Worksheet: The Marketing diary	This activity gives students the opportunity to work with a paper-based diary. The task contains a list of different items to be added to the diary.	Worksheet on CD-ROM	P2	Pages 232–234, 236–241
Outcome 2 Know how to operate office systems and equipment				
6.4 Introductory activity: What are they?	This quick quiz can be used as a reminder check on the terminology used when operating telephone equipment.		P3	Pages 241–245
6.5 Worksheet: Electronic diary	This activity uses Microsoft Outlook or similar software to ask students to consider issues relating to electronic diaries and their use.	Worksheet on CD-ROM, use of MS Outlook, etc.	P2, M1	Pages 236–241
6.6 Discussion activity: Telephone technique	Small group work will help students to work on different strategies to deal with customers by telephone.	Notebook	P2, M1	Pages 241–245
6.7 Worksheet: Office equipment	Students are asked within this task to consider the best use of equipment to help with a specific task. There is more than one possible answer, to allow students some flexibility in their answers.	Worksheet on CD-ROM	P4	Pages 248–251

© Harcourt Education 2006

Activity type and description	Delivery notes	Extra resources	Links to grading criteria	Links to textbook
6.8 Worksheet: Email	This poster activity asks students to inform their class peers about how to use different functions of email and about issues to be aware of, such as not opening attachments from unknown sources.	Worksheet on CD-ROM. Large sheets of paper, coloured pens.	P4, M2	Pages 245–248
6.9 Plenary activity: Wots wrong with the email?	A text-based email gives students the chance to think about the appropriate tone of emails compared to text messages. This could also provide an opportunity to consider the use of text messaging at work.		P4	Pages 245–248
6.10 Discussion activity: Which should you do first and why?	This version of an in-tray exercise gives students the chance to work with priorities and consider what should be done first. Comparing ideas within the class can provide an opportunity to consider different priorities that individuals have, based on the type of job that they do.		P4, M2	Pages 251–252
6.11 Research activity: Instruction manual	Writing an instruction manual requires students to think clearly about their own understanding of how a piece of equipment works. It would be useful to have other instruction manuals available to give students ideas about how to produce one.	Instruction manuals for equipment	P4, M2	Page 251
Outcome 3 Be able to organise and provide administrative support for meetings				
6.12 Introductory activity: Agenda for the Charity Planning Meeting	The items that should be on the Charity Planning Meeting Agenda have been placed in the wrong order. Students are asked to put them in the right order and type up the correct agenda for the meeting and consider what each of the headings mean.	Computer/word processor if possible	P5, M3	Pages 258–259
6.13 Worksheet: Which layout?	This activity requires students to match the description of the room layout to the appropriate layout given.	Worksheet on CD-ROM. Pens	P5	Page 262
6.14 Case study: Transcript of a Meeting	Students are given a transcript of a meeting and asked to provide a set of minutes based on the events that happened. At the end they are asked to describe the process and why minutes are necessary.		P5, M3	Pages 263–265

Activity type and description	Delivery notes	Extra resources	Links to grading criteria	Links to textbook
6.15 Research activity: Travel arrangements	Researching travel arrangements gives students the opportunity to work on their administrative skills by producing an itinerary.	Computer	P5, M3	Pages 265–266
6.16 Plenary activity: What went wrong?	This activity describes a meeting where things went wrong. Students need to spot the errors within the meeting and then make recommendations for how things should be done differently.	Paper and access to word processing software	P5, M3, D2	Pages 255–265
Outcome 4 Be able to demonstrate the procedures needed to process, retrieve and archive information				
6.17 PowerPoint presentation: Introduction to administration	This PowerPoint presentation gives an introduction to this administration unit.	Projector		Pages 268–275
6.18 Worksheet: Expense claim	This activity gives students the chance to process information in the form of an expense claim. It may be possible to extend this activity by comparing examples of expense claim forms available in the college or from work experience.	Worksheet on CD-ROM. Pens, calculator.	P6	Pages 131–132
6.19 Plenary activity: Paper-based filing system	Students are asked to put the procedures for paper-based systems in to the correct order.		P6	Pages 268, 270–275
6.20 Presentation activity: Electronic filing	This PowerPoint-based activity asks students to explore some of the issues related to electronic filing including the advantages and disadvantages of filing in this way.	Access to forms of electronic filing including the potential use of MS Access, access to PowerPoint and projector	P6	Pages 269–275

Unit 6 Activities

6.1 Introductory activity: What do the words mean?

Student book pages 232–234

To get you thinking about what is meant by administration and business support, you need to think about what the following words mean. In pairs, work out what they mean, using a dictionary to help you if you need to. Each word relates to the purpose of being able to provide business and administration support.

Word	Means … ?
Consistency	
Effective	
Supporting	
Administration	
Departmental functions	
Prioritising	
Organising	

Outcome 1

6.2 Research activity: Practical activities

**Student book
pages 232–234**

To understand what an administrator does in business you should experience some of the tasks that they might need to do.

1. Send an email message to your teacher, booking a meeting with them next week.
2. Write a letter on behalf of your class, booking a table at a local restaurant.
3. Research the arrangements for a hotel booking for two people at the end of the month in Bournemouth, and write this up as a leaflet to be given to your teacher.

Ask your teacher to look through your work. You should be careful to make sure that the spelling and layout of your communications are correct and that the words you use are polite and business-like.

6.3 Worksheet activity: The Marketing diary

**Student book
pages 232–234, 236–241**

See CD-ROM

6.4 Introductory activity: What are they?

Student book pages 241–245

In the boxes provided, explain what is meant by each of the following terms:

Call back	
Fax	
Conference call	
Forwarding a call	
Voice mail	
Organisational procedures for answering the phone	
Checking regularly for callers' messages	

6.5 Worksheet activity: Electronic diary

Student book pages 236–241

See CD-ROM

6.6 Discussion activity: Telephone technique

Student book pages 241–245

You are working as an administrator in a busy sales office with lots of important clients. These messages have been left on the office's telephone messaging service.

In small groups work out how you would deal with each message.

Message 1, left 4.00 yesterday

This is John Stiles, I am after a quote for a new fridge-freezer. I haven't decided which one I want yet but I am thinking of an American model somewhere around the £2,500 price range. Please could someone call me back.

Message 2, left 4.15 pm yesterday

This is Raafi Miah calling about the Salesman of the Year presentations in July. Please could you let me know your nominations so I can send out the invitations as soon as possible. My number is 773282.

Message 3, 4.30 pm yesterday

Its Greg, just reminding you that I won't be in the office tomorrow, if anyone needs me I can be contacted on my mobile.

Message 4, 4.35 yesterday

I need to get hold of Sarah urgently, I need to make a complaint about my washing machine. It has broken down already and caused a lot of damage to my kitchen floor. I am really annoyed as this is the second one you have sent out to me in as many weeks. Please can you let me know what is happening as soon as possible or I will be contacting my solicitor about getting compensation or going to the papers at the very least. Please phone me urgently, it is Mrs Smith on 892883.

Message 5, left 8.45 am this morning

This is Sarah, I am not coming in today as I am unwell. Can you let Rajesh know he needs to ring Mrs Sroa to give her the latest information on her order. She wants to know the delivery date and the latest price. Please can you ask Greg to give her a ring.

6.7 Worksheet activity: Office equipment

Student book pages 248–251

See CD-ROM

6.8 Worksheet activity: Email

Student book pages 245–248

See CD-ROM

6.9 Plenary activity: Wots wrong with the email

Student book pages 245–248

This email has been sent to the manager of a retail store where Josh Brown is employed as a sales assistant. Spot the errors in the email and suggest how Josh should make improvements.

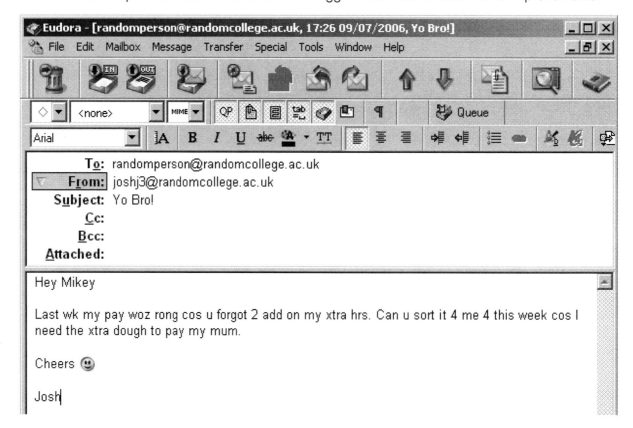

6.10 Discussion activity: Which should you do first and why?

Student book pages 251–252

1. File confidential documents
2. Type customer receipt
3. Order new stationery
4. Photocopy details of meeting next week, send out
5. Water office plants
6. Type up minutes from meeting last Friday
7. Phone L. Rossi to say new stock has arrived
8. Reply to email from Mrs Sekara complaining about poor service
9. Complete self-assessment task for meeting with JG tomorrow
10. Make appointment with dentist for next month

You have come into work and you have a list of these tasks to do for your department.

1. Put them in to order of what you would do first.
2. Compare your order of tasks with another member of your class
3. Were they the same or were they different? Explain your reasons why you chose to do the tasks in the order that you did.

6.11 Research activity: Instruction manual

Student book page 251

Write a three-page instruction manual for a piece of equipment in the office environment where you are studying – school, college, work experience or a part-time job. Use pictures, diagrams and text to explain how your colleagues should use the equipment safely and efficiently. Types of equipment you could use include

- photocopier
- laminator
- binder
- fax machine.

To work towards Merit level you will need to explain the features, functions and different purposes of the equipment in detail.

6.12 Introductory activity: Agenda for the Charity Planning Meeting

Student book pages 258–259

These agenda items have got all mixed up. Put them in the correct order and sign them as the Committees Secretary.

A meeting of the Charity Planning Committee will take place on 15 June at 11.30 in the Seminar Room at Angel College.

- Any other business
- Apologies for absence
- Appointment of co-ordinator
- Date and time of next meting
- Donations from students
- Grant arrangements from college
- Matters arising
- Minutes of the previous meeting
- Nominated charities
- Notice of meeting
- Publicity materials
- Visiting speaker

1 Type up the agenda correctly to be distributed to people going to the meeting.
2 What does each heading mean, and what is likely to be discussed at this point in the meeting?
3 Why are agendas so important in meetings?

6.13 Worksheet: Which layout?

Student book page 262

See CD-ROM

Providing business and administration support   145

6.14 Case study: Transcript of a meeting

Student book pages 263–265

The Meeting of the Animals Welfare Society took place on 2 May. Read through the transcript of the meeting and then write the minutes for it.

Neil: I'd like to welcome you all to our second meeting of the Animal Welfare Society Meeting. Our last meeting was on April 2 and I hope that you all received your minutes in the post

Alex: Yes I did, thank you, I wondered if they could be sent by email as I am worried about the amount of paper that we are sending out – could that be put on to the agenda for any other business for us to discuss.

Neil: Yes that would be good. Razoul, can you add that. Has anyone else got anything to add before we move on? (*Everyone shakes their heads.*) OK, Item 1 then – minutes of the last meeting. Are these true and accurate minutes of our last meeting? (*Everyone says yes in agreement.*) Well let's go through and check for any matters arising. At the last meeting it was agreed that Andrew would go and find out about other animal welfare groups in our area, how did that go, Andrew?

Andrew: It went well, I found out that there are three other main groups in this area, one concentrates on looking after the habitat of wild birds, another campaigning against animals being imported from abroad to be sold for dog and cat food, and finally a trust that makes sure that people on low incomes can get treatment for their sick animals if they need it.

Neil: Thank you for finding that out – anyone got any thoughts on those results?

George: I was sure that there was a charity that got involved with farm animal welfare near us as well. Does anyone else remember them and what were they called?

Evelyn: Yes I do George, I think they were called FAWS – the Farm Animal Welfare Society.

Neil: I suggest we action Evelyn to find out more about them and report back to our next meeting. Razoul, can you action her to do that in the minutes.

Razoul: Yes I will.

Neil: Are there any other matters arising from the minutes?

George: I managed to get a fund-raising pack sent from Head Office, it has all the kinds of information we were thinking of producing for our pack as examples. I have also asked for two other packs to be sent from other organisations but these have not been sent yet. I will let you all know when they arrive.

Neil: Razoul, please action George to bring more information to our next meeting. Any other matters arising? (*Everyone shakes their heads.*) OK, moving on to the agenda for today. There are two items to discuss. The Charity Fund-Raising Event and the petition against battery egg production. Starting with the Charity Fund-Raising Event, has anyone got any ideas?

Evelyn: I think we should have a football tournament with prizes for the winning team. I am sure there will be lots of interest in this event.

George: I think this is a good idea but it may not appeal to everyone, I really don't like football myself. I think it would be better to have some sort of quiz instead. It could have prizes.

Outcome 3   © Harcourt Education 2006

6.14 Case study: Transcript of a meeting (continued)

Andrew: Well last year at my college we raised over £250 by having a raffle, we asked local businesses to donate prizes in return for publicity. This meant we could raise a lot of money.

Evelyn: That does seem like a good idea but what is involved?

Andrew: Firstly you need to apply to the local council for a licence to run it, then you start writing out to local businesses or visiting asking for donations. Once everything is in, you start selling tickets, put up publicity and so on. It is quite easy really and can raise quite a lot of money.

Evelyn: Well I think that sounds like a good idea, especially as we only have limited time to get this done by.

Neil: Let's put it to the vote then – how many of us think that we should go with the raffle idea? Well, that is agreed unanimously. Andrew, please could you bring more information about the licences to the next meeting, Razoul, please could you action Andrew to do that in the Minutes, and Evelyn, would you like to find out about publicity materials?

Evelyn: Yes I would be happy to do that.

Neil: Razoul, please action Evelyn to bring back that information at our next meeting. Now on to Item 2 – the petition, how have you been getting on asking for names?

George: Well I managed to add another 20 names by taking it to my cricket club.

Andrew: I took it in to college and got another 10 names from people in my class. How many names do we have altogether?

Neil: At the last count it was 83, anyone else had any success?

Evelyn: I haven't been able to get any names as I have been really busy with other work but I am hoping to work really hard on it next week and get lots of extra names.

Neil: And what about you Razoul, how did you get on?

Razoul: I did really well. I got 30 names from my neighbours. That means we must be at 143 names. How many are we aiming for?

Neil: Well originally we aimed for 300 so could everyone please see if they could get some additional names and we will review it for next week. Razoul please action all of us to be working on this. Now does anyone have any other business?

Evelyn: I have one, I wanted to let you know about a Charity Market that is happening in October at the Community Centre. I think we should get a table there. The rental of the table for the event which is from 10 until 1 pm is £5 so we could sell items and make even more money for the charity. I have got the number of the lady organising it.

Neil: That sounds like a really good idea. Does everyone else agree? (*Everyone nods.*) So we will do that then – Evelyn please could you bring more information about the event next week and could we all think about the publicity for the event. Does anyone else have any thing else they want to discuss. (*Everyone shakes their head.*) OK, that's everything then. Our next meeting will be at the same time next week. Thank you everyone and see you next week.

When you have completed the set of minutes, explain how you produced the minutes and why it is so important to have minutes available from meetings.

6.15 Research activity: Travel arrangements

Student book pages 265–266

Miss Khan needs to go to a meeting in Broad Street, Birmingham, on the last day of next month.

1 Arrange travel from your college to Broad Street by train, and work out a suitable hotel that she can spend the night in the night before.

2 Type up an itinerary giving full details of the trip.

3 Give her directions to the hotel from the nearest train station to the hotel and work out the total costs that she is likely to have to pay out to get there.

4 Why is it so important to make sure Miss Khan has a clear itinerary for the meeting?

6.16 Plenary activity: What went wrong?

Student book pages 255–265

Look at the scenario below – what has gone wrong in this meeting? How could these problems have been avoided? Why is it so important to have good administrative support in meetings?

Jess arrived late for the meeting and apologised to everyone present. She was late because she couldn't remember where the meeting was being held and thought it was starting at 2.15 and not 2.00 this time. John had forgotten to send out the agenda before the meeting. He had been too busy, and just before he went home at 6 pm last night, had simply sent round a quick email to remind everyone that they were meeting.

John gave out the agenda by passing round a piece of paper to everyone. 'Sorry the agenda is a bit late this week. I was a bit busy this week,' he said.

Jane asked who was coming to the meeting – did anyone have a delegate list? 'Sorry,' said John, 'I knew there was something I had forgotten.'

'I know Javed was coming as he told me last week and he asked to have something put on the agenda for the meeting .... I can't remember what that was – does anyone else remember?' said Jess.

'Oh well,' John sighed, 'we can always add it as any other business!'

As it was now nearly 2.30, everyone was keen to press on. John thought his motto had always been 'start on time, finish on time', but he was now beginning to wonder. Javed arrived in a fluster: 'Sorry, got delayed, now where are we? Poppy won't be able to make it today as she has got flu.'

Finally everyone was ready to start and John officially opened the meeting. He had never been happy to be leading the meeting and being the administrator but no one else ever wanted to do either job. 'Did everyone bring their minutes with them to go through?' he said.

'Minutes? Minutes?' they all sighed back at him.... 'We never got any from the last meeting! It looks like we will have to go back over it all again.'

6.17 PowerPoint presentation: Introduction to administration

Student book pages 268–275

See CD-ROM

6.18 Worksheet: Expense claim

Student book pages 131–132

See CD-ROM

6.19 Plenary activity: Paper-based filing system

Student book pages 268, 270–275

These are the instructions for keeping paper-based files processed correctly. They are in the wrong order, so put them in the right order.

- Add the paper document to the file in the correct place – usually the most recent on top.
- Are there any problems with the paper that need replacing or repairing eg with tape?
- Is it complete and have paperclips been removed?
- Is it stapled in the right order for filing?
- Is the document ready for filing?
- Is this definitely the right file – second check?
- Place the file on a suitable surface ready to add the new document
- Put the file with the new document back into storage
- Take the file from its store
- Where is the file that the document is going to be stored in?

6.20 Presentation activity: Electronic filing

Student book pages 269–275

Find out about different types of electronic filing and how it works. Produce a PowerPoint presentation giving details about how electronic filing works and the advantages and disadvantages of using electronic filing at work.

Unit 6 Exemplar assignment

Assignment 6.1

Background to the Assignment

This assignment is aiming to help you achieve:

P1 Describe the purpose and types of business and administration support

P2 Operate a diary system

M1 Compare and contrast paper and electronic diary systems

You have been asked by a local businessman to investigate the role of business administration in the workplace. For this assignment, the first of three, you will need to produce a poster and information pack that can be used by the business man to display in his organisation or be given out to customers.

Task 1 (P1)

The purposes and types of business and administration support

For this task you will need to produce a detailed poster giving details about all the reasons why businesses need business and administration support and the types of support that this involves.

You will need to research your own ideas, based on work experience, your part-time job or work that you have carried out in your college. Some useful areas to consider to help you are:

- making sure everything is the same – consistency
- time
- helping managers
- organisation
- meetings
- documents
- travel
- event planning.

You will need to explain your poster to your teacher or other members of your class to show that you know what it means.

Task 2 (P2, M1)

Compare and contrast paper and electronic diary systems

The local business man in your area has been considering moving over from a paper-based diary system to an electronic one.

Produce an information pack to help him make his mind up about whether or not he should move over to a new system.

Find out as much information and include your sources of information in your pack.

a Describe, using real examples, how an electronic or paper based diary system works (P2)

Some possible areas to include are:

- entries to be made
- planning
- people involved
- communication
- implications of new entries.

Make sure you give an example of a working paper-based diary, to demonstrate that you can operate a diary.

b Explain how an electronic diary system is different from a paper-based system, again using real examples as much as possible (M1). Think about:

- access
- communication
- reminders
- being able to read it
- appointment clashes.

c Explain how a paper-based system has the same things as an electronic diary system, using real examples as much as possible (M1)

Use the example words above to help you.

Task 1

Business and Administration Support

What is it for?

It can help the business be more organised with its time because a support person is trained to do this

It can make a business produce things quicker eg typed documents

It allows managers to work on the business and not have to do all the telephone calls and letters

It can help a department run easily because they have a secretary to organise them for filing and meetings

What is it?

Typing paperwork before or after meetings

Making arrangements for meetings

Typing up other documents that are asked for

Looking after a diary so that everything is covered.

Putting through claims for expenses that the employees have put in.

Booking hotels and arranging transport

K Singh Assignment 6.1

Assessor feedback

Task 1 (above)

You have produced a good poster with information describing the role of administration and support at work. You did not have consistency on your poster. This is a really important reason for having administration support that we talked about in class. By having a certain way of doing things all the documents are laid out in the same way and therefore they are consistent.

Please add this to your poster before we go through it to check your understanding.

Task 2 (below)

Kirpal you have produced a really excellent piece of work describing how a paper-based diary system works and then clearly explaining the differences. I thought your work on electronic diaries was really good.

Your description for P2 was clear and you included an example. For M1 you described the differences in the text and also included a table at the end.

Your presentation was really good, including your layout. You are really showing the skills of an administrator to help you with this work.

Well done.

Diaries Information Pack by
K. Singh   Assignment 6.1

Paper Based Diary
A paper based diary is the usual kind of diary that you might find at home. There are lots of different types of paper diaries that you can use. Some are given that can be hung on the wall and some are called desk diaries

Wall diaries
These diaries are ones that you hang on the way. They sometimes show one month at a time so that you can see what is happening in that month straight away. This means that if something is happening later in the week or even in two weeks time you can see it. For wall diaries there are also ones that are called wall planners and these show the whole year or sometimes parts of the year but many months are shown which makes planning easier.

Desk diaries
These are diaries that live on your desk. They can be showing a whole week when the pages are open or sometimes they show a page per day. It depends on how much they need to write for how useful they are to a manager. Desk diaries can be kept on the desk or smaller ones ca be put in someone's pocket if they need to carry them around with them.

All types of paper based diaries are useful because a team in an office can see the diary on the wall or on the administrators desk and then can add things to the diary. This means things like having to go to a training session or a meeting. This helps the office to be organised so that there is always someone available at the office in case they are needed. People might also have a diary to plan things for themselves, they can write in what they should be doing to remind them. This can help them plan for meeting to be put at times so they reach them at the right time and not be arriving too later or too early.

In a paper diary an administrator will pass on information from the diary to the team involved to help them plan their day or week. They might book appointments with customers in the diary and then tell the team later. Sometimes if a workplace needs to have confidential things put in to the diary a manager may ask for an appointment to be put in to the diary but may ask the administrator to write booked in it instead of who it is with to help keep confidentiality so nobody knows who it is with. This is important if it is private.

Paper based diaries can also be used to tell where someone is if there is an emergency the administrator can look at the diary and see where someone is.

Sometimes appointments need to be changed so it is important that the diary and the people involved are told so that they both know what is happening. If they don't get enough notice it may mean that the meeting cannot happen. By having a good diary it should be that meetings are not booked at the same time, if only diary is used. The administrator should keep hold of the diary and make sure it is not lost. If it was lost the business might lose money because they wouldn't be able to book appointments or go to the ones they had already made. Without having a diary system it would be very difficult for a manager to organise their week because they wouldn't know when they should be doing things.

In a paper based diary the entries are written by hand with a pen or a pencil. Usually pencil is better in case things change. If pen is used then the administrator would need to use correcting fluid to change the entry and this might get messy if they need to keep changing things.

To show how a paper diary works I have put the morning appointments for a day into the diary of a shared office diary where 6 people are working.

```
Monday 20 June

9.00    Meeting with Miss Brown from C B Ltd (Rajesh)
        Sara to leave for business presentation about new materials in Coulsdon
        Rod, Mina, Jeff and Tom preparing latest sales forecast
10.20   Mina to have review appraisal with Jeff - booked out until 11.20
11.00   Rod to speak to Mrs Bridgewater about her latest order
11.00   Rajesh working on his sales forecasts
11.15   Tom booked out to travel to Chester
13.00   Lunchtime team briefing - Tom wont be available.
```

The diary that I have shown working is only for a morning but already it has six entries for one morning. This shows that I can operate a diary for six people but also how complicated it is.

Electronic Diaries
Some of the things about electronic diaries at the same as the paper based diary like appointments can be booked and people can know what they are going to do each day or each week. An electronic diary works like a paper diary with days and times but instead of it being kept centrally it can be viewed on a computer by lots of different people at once.

The entries are put in to the diary by typing them in. Lots of people use Microsoft Outlook to organise their diary. In outlook it is called a calendar. Appointments can be booked in and the times shaded.

The first difference between an electronic and paper diary is that if a mistake is made in the paper diary then it can be more difficult to see than using IT. The computer will give the user a warning that two things have been booked at the same time. A paper diary does not do that.

The second thing is that with an electronic diary a person does not have to have the actual diary with them. This is because someone in administration can change the diary and view it at any time but it can also be used by the person who needs it as well. This means that nobody has to look after the diary or lock it away. They can look themselves. Also because people cant get in without their passwords to the IT system, it is more secure as people who shouldn't be looking at the diary cannot view it.

Changing appointments is also easier online because they can just be deleted and a new one added by any of the people involved, the manager or the administrator. The diary can be carried around on a lap top and then be updated at any time the person is connected to the internet. The administrator can send an email to the person involved letting them know things have changed if this is needed or just make the changes for them.

Electronic diaries also are able to give reminders automatically. This means that when an appointment is coming up a message will be given to the person on their lap top. This helps them to get to their meeting on time as the reminder usually comes 15 minutes, 10 minutes or 5 minutes before the meeting.

Summary
To compare and contrast paper and electronic diaries I have made the table below

Differences	Paper Diary	Electronic Diary
Storage	With the administrator	Online so no worries about storage as on the computer
Easy to read	Written by hand so may be difficult to read	Typed so easy for everyone
Clashes	May not show clashes	Will give a warning if too appointments are booked at the same time
Access	Kept centrally so everyone needs to speak to the administrator about it	Able to be accessed from the PC anywhere internet linked
Confidentiality and security	Can be kept confidential with appointments written as booked rather than names. Has to be locked away to stop it being looked at by the wrong people	Only people with the right access on the computer can look at it.
Reminders	These need to be done by the administrator by phoning or leaving a note or list	The electronic diary will automatically remind the person about the appointment

These are all the things that are the same between paper and electronic diaries:
1. Appointments are put in.
2. People can be booked in to do things
3. It is possible to tell where people are and what they are doing
4. Plans can be made for what is happening
5. Changes can be made if an appointment needs to be changed
6. Tasks can be given to get the job done.

Unit 6 Resources

Additional resources that can be used to support student learning of this Unit are:

Textbooks

Carysforth, C. and Neild, M., *BTEC First Business* (Heinemann, 2006)

Fardon, M., Nuttall, C. and Prokopiw, J., *GCSE Applied Business* (Osborne Books, 2002)

Websites

There are lots of websites available to help in the area of administration. Some useful sites that may provide additional information and ideas include:

www.bized.ac.uk	Bized business education site
www.cfa.uk.com	The Council for Administration (CfA) — the National Sector Setting Body for Business and Administration. It is responsible for defining and promoting excellence in business and administration skills and practice across all industry sectors

Unit 7 Personal selling

Unit overview

Unit 7 is a specialist unit for the BTEC First Certificate and BTEC First Diploma qualifications in Business. The unit gives students the chance to look into the world of personal selling from practical and theoretical perspectives.

Students are first introduced to the concept of why personal selling exists and the relevant legislation that impacts on the world of selling.

They then need to demonstrate the ability to prepare for selling, and through this activity are able to work to differing levels, depending on the independent research and application they show.

There is scope within this unit for self-reflection and role-playing. Case study material will help students to get ideas about how personal selling should take place and the processes involved. Assessed role-plays help students to provide evidence that this has taken place.

These role-plays consider personal selling skills, the need to close sales and how to deal with customer objections.

The final part of the unit looks at the reasons for recording information and how after-sales care and follow-up should take place.

Suggested activities

The table on the following pages shows how activities in this Assessment and Delivery Resource cover the four different outcomes of the Unit. There are a variety of tasks including discussion material, worksheets, case studies and presentation material.

The research tasks have been prepared to allow students to gather evidence in note form to help them produce their own work.

How this unit will be assessed

To gain a Pass, learners will need to:

P1 describe the purpose of sales personnel and the knowledge and skills required for personal selling

P2 describe the legislation that affects personal selling

P3 describe the preparation needed to support personal selling in two different situations

P4 demonstrate personal selling skills and processes in two different situations

P5 demonstrate the process of closing sales in two different situations

P6 demonstrate how to respond to customers' objections in two different situations

P7 describe the reasons for following up sales and recording customer information.

To gain a Merit requires learners to complete all the Pass requirements plus the Merit requirements, where they need to:

M1 demonstrate an independent approach to a major part of their work, showing confident and effective personal selling skills

M2 explain how legislation might affect personal selling in two different situations

M3 compare and contrast the personal selling skills and processes used in two different situations.

To gain a Distinction requires a learner to complete all the Pass and Merit requirements plus the Distinction requirement, where they need to:

D1 demonstrate excellent and confident personal selling in at least three different situations

D2 evaluate the preparation to support personal selling and the personal selling skills and processes carried out in two different situations

Learning outcomes

The unit is based on the following learning outcomes

1. Understand the purpose of sales personnel
2. Know how to prepare for personal selling
3. Be able to demonstrate personal selling skills and processes
4. Understand sales closing techniques and how to identify customers' objections.

At-a-glance

Activity type and description	Delivery notes	Extra resources	Links to grading criteria	Links to textbook
Outcome 1 Understand the purpose of sales personnel				
7.1 Introductory activity: Car selling	This activity encourages students to think about why personal selling is really important and what a car seller actually does.		P1	Pages 278–282
7.2 Case study: Dixons and Currys	A case study that asks students to consider why Currys have continued to use personal selling for their higher-priced items, whereas Dixons have closed their shops and now only sell online.	Internet access	P1	Pages 278–282
7.3 Discussion activity: Which of these is most important?	The qualities of a successful sales person are put in order by the students and they can compare their results to see if they all agree on what makes a perfect sales person.		P1	Pages 278–282
7.4 Research activity: Which law?	Brief scenarios are given and students need to identify an Act of Parliament that governs each situation.	Information about the Acts	P2	Pages 282–285
7.5 Plenary activity: Legal effects	Two scenarios are given and students using hints are asked to describe and explain how the law affects selling in each of these situations.	Information about the Acts	P2, M2	Pages 282–285
Outcome 2 Know how to prepare for personal selling				
7.6 Introductory activity: Telephone Preference Service	The role of the TPS is examined and students asked to consider the effect of consumers asking for their telephone numbers not to be used, and the implications of having call centres operating from abroad.	Newpaper articles, websites	P2, P3	Pages 289, 291
7.7 Research activity: Planning your sales talk	A script is designed by the student for how they should open a conversation with a potential customer. This could be enhanced by including the closing part of the process, but at this stage the opening and introduction is concentrated upon.	Paper, pens, PC	P3, P4	Pages 289–299

Personal selling **157**

Activity type and description	Delivery notes	Extra resources	Links to grading criteria	Links to textbook
7.8 Research activity: Sandwich questionnaire	Conducting research is an important part of knowing your customer so students are asked to collect data on the new 'Hot Toasties' business to then relate the information to personal selling techniques that could be used.	Additional props or material added for 'Hot Toasties'	P3, M1	Pages 289–299
Outcome 3 Be able to demonstrate personal selling skills and processes				
7.9 Introductory worksheet: Level of personal selling	Students are asked how businesses use sales representatives, and the benefits of using personal selling.	Worksheet on CD-ROM	P4, M3	Pages 301–308
7.10 Case study: The Pampered Chef	A case study that looks at the way that Pampered Chef have expanded by using personal selling in a similar way to other companies such as Tupperware or Body Shop at Home. Evaluating this case study can give data for D2.	More information and websites about the Pampered Chef	P4, M3, D2	Pages 304–308
7.11 Case study: Carpetright	A case study using Carpetright is given to allow students to think about why personal selling is important when buying or selling carpet.	A visit to a Carpetright or a representative coming in to class would be useful, Internet access	P4, M3	Pages 304–308
7.12 Role-play activity: Selling techniques	A practical role play situation with a checklist is given to allow students to play the part of seller, customer and observer. This would make an excellent pre-assessment activity that could also benefit from being videoed if students are happy with this.	Video equipment, props to be used as part of the role-play	P4, P5, P6, P7, M3, D1	Pages 301–308
Outcome 4 Understand closing techniques and how to identify customers' objections				
7.13 Introductory activity: Closing a sale	This activity gives students the opportunity to think of possible answers to objections that a customer may give when trying to close a sale.		P6	Pages 312–313

© Harcourt Education 2006

Activity type and description	Delivery notes	Extra resources	Links to grading criteria	Links to textbook
7.14 Worksheet: Timings	This activity asks student to think about the amount of time that needs to be invested in persuading a customer to buy a product or service and how quickly the customer may make a decision.	Worksheet on CD-ROM	P5, M3	Pages 314–315
7.15 Research activity: Personal selling slogans	This activity asks students to think of a slogan that could help sales people to increase sales and develop selling skills.		P5, M1	Pages 312–315
7.16 Discussion activity: Your own objections	Students are asked to consider what would stop them purchasing a product so that they can think of ways to overcome their own objections.	Paper to make chart	P6	Pages 312–315
7.17 Research activity: Customer care	This activity asks students to find out the different processes that businesses use as part of customer care.	Internet access	P7, M3	Pages 315–316
7.18 Plenary activity: Information mind-map	This activity asks students to think about the type of information a business would need to keep on its customers, how that information is stored and what it is used for.		P7, M3	Page 317
7.19 Powerpoint presentation: Recording customer details	This PowerPoint presentation considers the records that businesses keep and how they are used.	Projector	P7	Page 317

At-a-glance

Unit 7 Activities

7.1 Introductory activity: Car selling

Student book pages 278–282

A car seller is a really important person in relation to personal selling. For each of the categories below, write how a car seller can help with each of these tasks.

Area for consideration	Explanation
How can a car seller increase sales?	
How might a car seller up-sell?	
How does a car seller make sure a business remains competitive?	
How does a car seller provide information and services to customers?	
How does a car seller help with customer care?	
How does a car seller provide feedback to his employer and what kind of feedback do they give?	

Outcome 1

7.2 Case study: Dixons and Currys

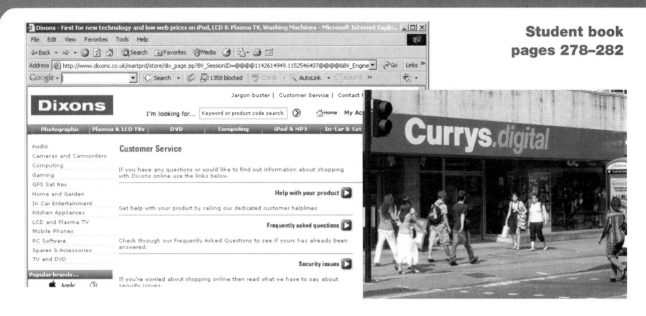

Student book pages 278–282

In April 2006 the owner of the Dixons and Currys group of companies announced that many Dixon's shops would be closed and others would have their name changed to Currys. This is because smaller electrical goods that Dixons traditionally sell, such as MP3 players or iPods, are more commonly being bought over the Internet from the Dixons website. Currys stores, on the other hand, are still going to sell larger and more expensive goods, with personal sellers available in store.

1. Why do you think personal selling is more important for expensive goods than it is for cheaper goods?
2. What are the advantages of having a personal seller to present goods in store?
3. What might be the disadvantages of using a personal seller, or the additional costs involved compared to online selling?

7.3 Discussion activity: Which of these is most important?

Student book pages 278–282

Put these qualities in the order of which you think is the most important for a sales person to have.

- Self-motivation
- Ability to learn quickly
- Be able to talk to a wide variety of people
- Be able to keep up to date
- Be a quick thinker
- Be passionate about their work
- Be organised
- Be keen to earn money by receiving commission on sales
- Be able to speak clearly
- Be flexible
- Be confident about themselves
- A positive outlook
- Be the kind of person who doesn't give up.

Check your answers with others in your group to see if you have all chosen the same things as being the most important.

Personal selling 161

7.4 Research activity: Which law?

Student book pages 282–285

Some pieces of legislation influence the way that buying and selling takes place. Use the scenarios below to work out which piece of legislation deals with the issue given. You have been given the scenario plus extra detail. In the boxes on the right, say which piece of legislation applies in each scenario.

Scenario	Detail	Applicable law
Buy a packet of crisps 100g in weight	pack contains only 50g	
Buy a washing machine	leaking on first day of use	
Buy child seat for car	no instructions given for fitting	
Buy TV	sign agreement to pay £50 per month	
Take car for repairs	problem not fixed, worse than before	

7.5 Plenary activity: Legal effects

Student book pages 282–285

Describe and explain how law affects selling in these two situations:

1
An electrical retailer selling products to the public from a catalogue

Hints
- Sale of Goods Act
- quality
- fit for the purpose
- Consumer Protection Act
- Product Safety
- Trades Descriptions Act

2
A sales representative calling on customers showing samples of the product that will be supplied

Hints
- Sale of Goods
- quality
- bulk must match sample
- Consumer Protection Act
- Consumer Credit Act

Outcome 1

© Harcourt Education 2006

7.6 Plenary activity: Telephone Preference Service

Student book pages 289, 291

The Telephone Preference Service came into existence as a result of The Privacy and Electronic Communications Regulations 2003, which makes it illegal to phone people in order to promote new products or services if they have registered with this service. This means that businesses are breaking the law if they telephone people or businesses who have asked not to be contacted.

If a large number of people continue to sign up to this service, it may prevent companies from using telemarketing, i.e. using the phone to let them know about their products or services.

One way some companies have decided to get around this problem is to use call centres based abroad, which do not have to follow UK law. This means they can currently phone customers who have asked not to be contacted.

1. How might the use of the Telephone Preference Service make it difficult for businesses to identify potential customers?
2. How might it make it easier?
3. What is the impact of call centres being based abroad on UK customers – how might they feel about this?

7.7 Research activity: Planning your sales talk

Student book pages 289–299

Write a script/plan for you to start the selling process with a new customer coming in to the trainer store where you work.

1. How would you start a conversation with them?
2. Which information should you tell them first?
3. How can you find out their needs?
4. What could you say to encourage them to think about buying your trainers?

When you have finished, practise your script on a member of your class and ask them for comments on what went well and what could be improved.

7.8 Research activity: Sandwich questionnaire

Student book pages 289–299

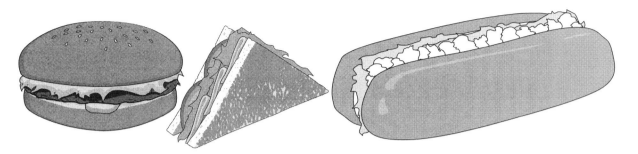

Find out the sandwich buying habits of students in your class. You will need to find out what persuades them to buy a sandwich, where they would buy it from, how much money they might need to pay, how much information they might need about the product before they buy it, and so on.

1 Use a questionnaire to collect the information, and then work out how you could use personal selling techniques to persuade them to use a new sandwich service called 'Hot Toasties'.

2 How could you persuade them to buy 'Hot Toasties', and how could you encourage them to upgrade their choice using upselling to help you?

3 Which skills would you need to use to persuade them to switch from their usual choice?

7.9 Introductory worksheet: Level of personal selling

Student book pages 301–308

See CD-ROM

7.10 Case study: The Pampered Chef

Student book pages 304–308

The Pampered Chef is a business that makes extensive use of personal selling as a way to gain sales and let people know about its kitchen gadget products. Like other party planning businesses, such as Tupperware or Body Shop at Home, the Pampered Chef personal selling technique works by giving demonstrations in party hosts' homes, using the equipment that the organisation is trying to sell.

A party will involve a display being put up in a host's home to show all the possible products that are then on offer. The host is a person who has freely offered to have the party in their home and is responsible for inviting all the guests. A table will be placed in the centre of the room and the representative will show how to make a recipe using the equipment being offered. Once the recipe has been completed the people attending the party are asked if they would like to try what is on offer before additional products are handed round for people to look at and decide if they would like to buy them.

The business was launched in the US more than 21 years ago, but has only been in the UK since 2000. Since this time it has grown and grown into a successful US and UK enterprise.

For more information go to www.pamperedchef.com

Using the information provided and by researching more into Pampered Chef:

1. Describe the preparation needed to support selling for Pampered Chef.
2. Compare the personal selling techniques used by them compared to those used by a kitchen shop.
3. How well do you think Pampered Chef representatives need to prepare in order to sell effectively, and how important are the skills they need to do this?
4. How can you measure the success of Pampered Chef as a business when thinking about the techniques it uses?

7.11 Case study: Carpetright

Student book pages 304–308

For more information go to
www.carpetright.co.uk

Carpetright is a national chain of shops selling carpets and rugs. To purchase a carpet a customer goes into the shop with the measurements of their room and then discusses their requirements with the salesperson.

As part of the service, the salesperson can make recommendations about different types of carpets, and about special offers and when they end, and can arrange fitting with carpet fitters.

Carpetright also offer a home quote service, where a carpet consultant can go round to a customer's house and give them a free quote about how much a new carpet would cost. The consultant is also able to offer them extra advice in the home about different types of carpet and what would go well with the room.

1. Why do you think Carpetright choose to use salespeople operating personal selling in this way?
2. What are the advantages of having a salesperson giving individual advice to a customer?
3. What might the disadvantages be?

7.12 Role-play activity: Selling techniques

Student book pages 301–308

Here you are given three different role-plays to carry out. Get into groups of three – you will need to prepare to sell the products and then ask one person in the group to be the seller, one to be the customer and the third person to write down comments about how the seller did. Each of the sellers will need to prepare for their role by preparing materials and finding out about possible products to talk about.

Remember to be helpful to the seller by saying what they did well, but also by giving suggestions on how the person could improve by using the checklist given below. You will need three copies of the checklist – one for each scenario.

Scene 1: mobile phone

A sales person in a mobile phone shop and a customer has come in wanting to buy a phone for their mum as a present. They only have a limited amount of money.

Scene 2: holiday

Two different short breaks are organised by the college during half term, one is as part of a study week, the other is a team building challenge to help with learning about leadership.

7.12 Role-play activity: Selling techniques (continued)

Scene 3: health club

Two different memberships of a health club – one is for a service that includes just the gym during college hours, the other is for use at any time and includes the sauna and steam room. The customer is thinking about gym membership.

Scene number:	
Describing the service that is available to go with the product.	
Responding to objections or reasons why the customer doesn't want the product	
Closing sales	
Recording customer information – follow up?	
Greeting and introducing the product	
Get the customer's interest	
Identifying the customer's needs	
Displaying the product or giving information	
Describing the product	
Giving different product options	

1 At the end of the role-plays, compare and contrast the different techniques that were used in these situations.

2 Consider how well-prepared each of the sellers was – how important was preparation?

7.13 Introductory activity: Closing a sale

Student book pages 312–313

Closing a sale is really important as this is part of the process where customers actually buy the product or service. Sometimes customers will think of reasons, known as objections, for why they can't buy an item. Good personal selling tries to reduce these objections by giving customers something else to think about or different ways of looking at the objections.

For each of the objections below think of a way that the customer could be persuaded to buy the product or the objection be reduced in size. The first one has been done for you.

Objection	Possible responses
The item cost more than the customer wanted to spend	It is of a high quality so it is worth paying that little bit extra. It is possible to pay in instalments so that makes it easier to afford
The customer is in no rush to buy today	
The customer wants to see how much competitors are selling the item for	
The item is not the right colour – they would prefer it in orange	
The brand is one they have never heard of and they are worried it may not be reliable	

7.14 Worksheet: Timings

Student book pages 314–315

See CD-ROM

Outcome 4

7.15 Research activity: Personal selling slogans

Student book pages 312–315

Some organisations use slogans or acronyms to help them to get sales people to think of ways that they can sell more products or services.

In the late 1980s, one fast-food chain used the WINNING slogan to help their waiting staff to encourage customers to buy more. This was a form of personal selling that gave customers additional information about products and also encouraged them to order more, leading to increased sales.

Each element of WINNING helped the sales staff to think about the selling process and what they needed to do.

- W – welcome the customer
- I – invite them to look at a menu
- N – now offer them a drink
- N – now take their food order
- I – inquire about their meal
- N – now go for the dessert order
- G – thanks and good bye.

Each stage of WINNING helped staff to think about how to increase their sales.

Now it is your turn. Think of a product or service that you have used in the past or you would like to use, and come up with a slogan or acronym that would help sales people to personally sell that product. Demonstrate to members of your class how this acronym or slogan could be used to develop personal selling skills.

Outcome 4

7.16 Discussion activity: Your own objections

Student book pages 312–315

You have thought about ways to reduce the objections of customers, but what are the most common objections in your class for a given product?

Imagine you need to sell a pair of jeans for £50 to other students in your class. They are made by a new designer from Spain and are good-quality. Use the table to find out the different numbers of objections that may result from members of your class thinking about buying this product. Ask members of your class to tell you the one biggest objection that they are likely to have.

Objection	Number of people with this objection
Cost	
Timing	
Needing to find out what other jeans manufacturers are offering	
Type of design	
Unheard-of brand	
Other objection	

1. Produce a chart showing the most common objection, and then think of ways that you could try and reduce the top three objections.
2. How much of this is within your control and how much is outside your control?

Outcome 4 © Harcourt Education 2006

7.17 Research activity: Customer care

Student book pages 315–316

For each of the following businesses find out what the businesses do for their customers in terms of delivery, customer service, follow-up and complaints.

You may find it useful to split your class into small groups and then share your results with everyone.

Business	Product delivery	Customer satisfaction monitoring and feedback	Follow-up call after sales	Complaints procedure
Ocado www.ocado.com				
B and Q www.bandq.co.uk or www.diy.co.uk				
SCS www.scssofas.co.uk				
Argos www.argos.co.uk				
Riverford www.riverford.co.uk				

Outcome 4

Personal selling   171

7.18 Plenary activity: Information mind-map

Student book page 317

Using the diagram below to help you, think of all the different information that a business may need to record about its customers.

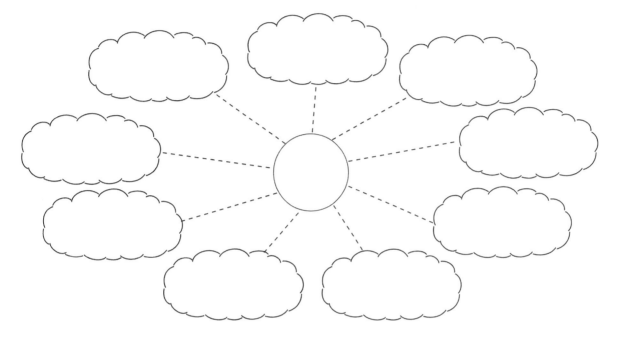

1 For each type of information, explain how that information could be used in future.
2 What might limit the amount that is used, or decide whether it is used at all?

7.19 PowerPoint presentation: Recording customer details

Student book page 317

See CD-ROM

Outcome 4   © Harcourt Education 2006

Unit 7 Exemplar assignment

Assignment 7.2

Background to the assignment

This assignment is aiming to help you achieve:

P2 Describe the legislation which affects personal selling

M2 Explain how legislation might affect personal selling in two different situations.

You have been asked to give a presentation on the different laws that affect personal selling. Within your presentation, using either cards or PowerPoint, you will need to include the main laws that affect personal selling. Then, for the Merit work, you will need to explain how these laws will affect the way that the personal selling tasks place.

Please read both sets of presentation notes before you decide whether to go for P2 or P2 and M2.

Presentation to cover P2

Within your presentation you will need to *describe* the different laws that affect personal selling when you buy something from one of the places listed below

- Beauty counter in a chemist such as Boots
- Car seller
- Buying electrical equipment from a store such as Curry's
- Photography studio
- Credit card being sold on the High Street
- Shoe shop

The legislation that you will need to include in your presentation is

- Consumer Credit Act 1987
- Consumer Protection Act 1987
- Sales of Goods Act 1979 and 1995
- Supply of Goods and Services Act 1982
- Trades Description Act 1967.

You should also include any other legislation that you find out about when you are researching your idea.

Presentation to cover P2 and M2

When you have described the different laws that will affect the personal selling at one of the places described you then need to explain how these laws affect personal selling in *two different* situations by giving examples. You can use the same list above to help you or different examples if you know them.

Slide 1

Legislation affecting personal selling for Curry's Electrical Stores

J Morris
Unit 7 BTEC First

Slide 2

The main pieces of legislation affecting personal selling of electrical equipment

Consumer Credit Act 1987
- Sales of Goods Act 1979 and 1995
- Supply of Goods and Services Act 1982
- Trades Description Act 1967

Slide 3

Consumer Credit Act 1987

- This piece of law controls the way that a business can offer credit. Credit means having something and then paying for it later. A business has to give a written agreement, what it says in the agreement like the amount of interest they need to pay and time for the customer to change their mind.

Slide 4

Consumer Protection Act 1987

This law means that businesses must produce safe products so if something needs to be put together it needs to have fitting instructions with it.

It must be safe to sell or the business people could go to prison if it is not.

Student's work — PowerPoint presentation

Slide 5

Sale of Goods Act

This act makes sure that all goods that are sold by a business to a consumer are

Fit for the purpose that they are bought for
Satisfactory quality
Must match a sample if sold in a sample

Slide 6

Supply of Goods and Services Act 1982

This act means that the service or products must be fit for the purpose that they are for for example a car hire business must provide a safe car and provide a satisfactory service to go with it.

Slide 7

Trades Description Act 1967

Something that is sold by its description must match the description eg a holiday being sold must match what the brochure says about it.

Slide 8

- The End
- Any Questions

Witness statement for J Morris

Performance indicator

P2 Description of relevant legislation

You have given a presentation on Currys but have not related the pieces of law to Curry's at all. Your answers were general in terms of law and did not relate to personal selling.

With the Consumer Credit Act, for example, you need to describe how Currys customers might buy expensive electrical products such as televisions on credit and need to be given details about the interest rate in a store, the amount of the monthly payments, the amount of time a customer may have to change their mind about the order and so on. Please look at this presentation again.

M2 Explanation of the effect for two different organisations

Not attempted. To go for M2 you need to relate and explain your answers to Currys and another relevant business. Remember you need to explain the effect on personal selling eg for Currys and the Consumer Credit Act the personal seller would need to make sure that the agreement was clearly explained to the customer and that they understood what was meant by it so this means it is likely to take longer to sell a large item like this to a customer. They may also need to run a credit check on the customer so they would need to explain how this is done.

General information on the layout of the presentation, questions asked or feedback on presentation skills

Your presentation was very good and you were confident. Try and improve the content of your slides by relating them to Currys more and by not including too much detail on them so you use them as a prompt rather than reading from them.

Resubmission of presentation needed. P2 part achieved and M2 not attempted.

Unit 7 Resources

Additional resources that can be used to support student learning of this Unit are:

Textbooks

Carysforth, C. and Neild, M., *BTEC First Business* (Heinemann, 2006)

Fardon, M., Nuttall, C. and Prokopiw, J., *GCSE Applied Business* (Osborne Books, 2002)

Wall, J. and Wales, N, *Nuffield–BP Business and Economics for GCSE* (2nd edn, Collins, 2001)

Websites

There are lots of websites available to help. Some useful sites that may provide additional information and ideas include:

www.bized.ac.uk	Bized business education site
www.tpsonline.org.uk	Telephone Preference Service
www.sellingpower.com	Selling Power website with news and activities

© Harcourt Education 2006

Unit 8 Doing business online

Unit overview

Unit 8 is a specialist unit for the BTEC First Certificate and BTEC First Diploma qualifications in Business. The unit gives students the chance to look into the world of online business and to examine the benefits and issues that enterprises face when trading in this way.

Students are asked to consider why and how different businesses trade online by examining three different case studies in detail. They then go on to consider the ways that costs in terms of financial, staffing and marketing can be reduced in order to make businesses better able to compete, whether they are large or small.

Students are asked to consider some of the planning and implementation issues that might affect a business thinking about going online and, at Distinction level, make recommendations on whether or not a particular business should consider going online. For Merit work it is recommended that students use the same business through the three Merit criteria, but this is not essential.

The benefits of an online presence are looked at in detail as the final part of the unit including the benefits of having a presence in the online market with its 24 hour access and the ability to gain customers who may previously been unable to be contacted eg those with mobility issues or customers in other countries.

This unit gives students the operating to consider issues facing modern businesses and keep up to date with the latest trends in technological developments and buying patterns online.

Suggested activities

The table on the following page shows how activities in this Assessment and Delivery Resource cover the four different outcomes of the Unit. There are a variety of tasks including discussion material, worksheets, case studies and presentation material.

The research tasks have been prepared to allow students to gather evidence in note form to help them produce their own work.

How this unit will be assessed

To gain a Pass, learners will need to:

P1 describe three different business organisations and activities operating online

P2 describe the planning and implementation issues a business organisation would need to consider to go online

P3 prepare information on the operational issues and risks for a business organisation operating online

P4 describe the staffing, financial and distribution issues that a business organisation operating online should consider

P5 describe the benefits to a business organisation marketing a product or service online.

To gain a Merit requires learners to complete all the Pass requirements plus the Merit requirements, where they need to:

M1 explain the planning and implementation issues for a business organisation going online

M2 analyse the advantages and disadvantages of the operational issues and risks for a business organisation planning to go online

M3 explain the potential benefits for a business planning to go online.

To gain a Distinction requires a learner to complete all the Pass and Merit requirements plus the Distinction requirement, where they need to:

D1 make and justify recommendations for a business organisation considering going online

D2 suggest ways in which a business could prepare for, and overcome, some of the operational risks associated with an online presence.

Learning outcomes

The unit is based on the following learning outcomes:

1. Understand different online business activities
2. Know the benefits of an online business presence
3. Understand the operation of an online business
4. Understand the business feasibility of going online.

© Harcourt Education 2006

At-a-glance

Activity type and description	Delivery notes	Extra resources	Links to grading criteria	Links to textbook
Outcome 1 Understand different online business activities				
8.1 Case study: British Airways	This case study examines the use of online services and how they can cut costs and improve the passenger experience.		P1	Pages 322–329
8.2 Case study: Playmonday.com	This case study examines how this new lottery website makes use of reduced costs and secure payment to allow customers to make choices about who their lottery money goes to.	Internet access	P1	Pages 322–329
8.3 Plenary activity: Does it matter?	This discussion asks students to consider whether it is important to have a passive, interactive or dynamic website.	Internet access	P1, D1	Pages 326–329
Outcome 2 Understand the business feasibility of going online				
8.4 Introductory activity: Benefits to business	This set of guided questions asks students to think of the benefits of online trading themselves. They can be related to one specific business or a number of different businesses.		P5, M3	Pages 331–337
8.5 Case study: Dixons and Currys and …	Dixons are moving towards online trading only as the stores are rebranded to become Currys. This means that Currys will target larger white goods and Dixons will target online purchases of small items such as MP3 players and iPods. Students are asked to look at other businesses with e-tailing as well as retailing presences.	Pens, or PC if completed online	P5, M2	Pages 331–337
8.6 Discussion activity: Lowering costs	One of the key benefits of trading online is cost reduction. This activity asks students to explain clearly, and make judgements about, how this can be done.	Pens	P5, M3, D1	Pages 331–337

Doing business online

Activity type and description	Delivery notes	Extra resources	Links to grading criteria	Links to textbook
8.7 Worksheet: Company websites	This gapped piece of text gives details about business benefits and issues from having a company website.	Worksheet on CD-ROM. Pens	P5	Pages 331–337
8.8 Discussion activity: Who benefits?	Dealing with accessibility issues, this worksheet asks students to consider the additional customers a business could expect to attract and how they could benefit from this additional trade.	Pens	P5, M3	Pages 331–337
Outcome 3 Understand the operation of an online business				
8.9 Research activity: Paying online	Looking at the advantages and disadvantages of different methods of payment online allows students to consider operational issues. Text messaging is a new and popular method to take payments, but what are the issues?	Internet access	P3, P4	Pages 339–342, 346–348
8.10 Research activity: Fraud on the Internet	Seven types of fraud are considered, and students are asked to think about any types of online fraud they have experienced directly or indirectly. Reminders about chain emails, etc., as part of Internet safety training can be useful at this point.	Internet access	P3, M2	Pages 339–342
8.11 Worksheet: The most serious problem?	This activity asks students to consider which are the most serious issues for someone running and maintaining a website – out-of-date information, missing links, etc.? They should judge what they feel needs to be put to the top of the priority list.	Worksheet on CD-ROM.	P3, M2, D2	Pages 342–346
8.12 Research activity: Coping with unexpected demand	Sometimes businesses have to cope with unexpected demand, e.g. the Inland Revenue website failing due to demand and Amazon not being able to get orders out in time for Christmas 2004. These are real issues for businesses and it is difficult to anticipate demand online.	Internet access	P4	Pages 343–344, 346
8.13 Worksheet: Distribution	This activity asks students to consider how they can purchase different products and the way that those products are ordered and then received by them.	Worksheet on CD-ROM.	P4	Pages 348–350

© Harcourt Education 2006

Activity type and description	Delivery notes	Extra resources	Links to grading criteria	Links to textbook
8.14 Plenary activity: Staffing	This activity considers the change in the type of work that is likely to be available in the future and the way that online business can reduce the number of staff required by an organisation.	Internet access	P4, M2	Pages 344–346
Outcome 4 Know the benefits of an online business presence				
8.15 PowerPoint presentation: Online benefits	This PowerPoint presentation gives some useful tips and pointers for students the benefits of being online.		P5, M3	Pages 353–360
8.16 Worksheet: Petra's Pizza	Petra is thinking about starting up an online part of her business – students are asked to consider the stages she needs to go through, with prompts detailing the issues for her particular business.	Worksheet on CD-ROM.	P2, M1	Pages 356–360
8.17 Research activity: The pizza market	Researching into the market reminds students of the different possible levels of website interactivity, by looking into the pizza market in their area. They are likely to find large differences in website availability, and should be encouraged to question why this is.	Internet access	P2, M1	Pages 356–358, 326–329
8.18 Worksheet: It's all in a name	This activity asks student to guess, from the domain names alone, the type of services that are offered: then the students look up those websites. Extension material could be to ask students to consider the importance of domain names and the advantages and disadvantages of having an unusual or wacky name.	Worksheet on CD-ROM. Internet access	P2, M1	Pages 331–332
8.19 Plenary activity: Should Petra go online?	A final look back at Petra to be completed after all the other exercises. Students are asked to give reasons for her going online, reasons against and then a final judgement.		P5, M3, D1	Pages 353–360

Unit 8 Activities

8.1 Case study: British Airways

Student book pages 322–329

British Airways make extensive use of online business. By allowing customers to make their bookings directly with British Airways online they are able to save costs and give better customer service.

Customers can choose the flight that they want, based on the price that they choose, up to a year before they fly. They receive an e-ticket that they print out on their own computer (see the example on the next page). They can save money by booking early, and British Airways can benefit by receiving their payment much sooner.

Using the reference number and ticket information, you can go to Manage My Booking on www.ba.com at any time to:

- view your itinerary
- request a specific seat
- notify BA of special dietary requirements
- make changes to or cancel your booking
- find out about Online Check-in and BA's Self-Service Check-in kiosks
- email your itinerary to friends, family or colleagues
- view BA's destination and events guide
- add your Executive Club number (or other frequent flyer number) to your booking

Online check-in allows passengers to print out their own boarding pass, which has a barcode on it so that security checks can be made. This saves the passenger time as they can print it themselves, but also saves British Airways money as they don't have to pay for boarding passes to be printed.

By using the additional services listed above, the customer is likely to spend less time queuing at the airport, and feel much happier about the flight and service that they receive from BA.

1. What are the benefits to British Airways of using e-tickets and online check-ins?
2. What are the benefits to customers of British Airways of using both?
3. Are there any possible issues with using this type of booking service?

8.1 Case study: British Airways (continued)

An example of an e-ticket

Dear Customer,

We have sent you this email to provide you with:

- Your e-ticket receipt - itinerary and payment information
- Baggage information
- Managing or making changes to your booking
- Check-in options
- How to contact us
- Other service and legal information, including conditions of contract

---

YOUR E-TICKET RECEIPT – ITINERARY AND PAYMENT INFORMATION

You will not receive or need a separate paper ticket for this booking at any time.

We advise you to take this document with you, as you may need to present it at immigration or security when you travel.

Passengers: Mr Bob Brown and Mr C Hopper

British Airways booking reference: YG257YKG

Flight number: BA7948
From: Gatwick (London) Terminal N
To: Inverness
Depart: 12 Jul 2006 19:50
Arrive: 12 Jul 2006 21:45
Class: Domestic
Operated by: BA CONNECT
Booking status: Confirmed

On BA Connect, Iberia and Aer Lingus, food and drink is available for purchase onboard. BA Connect flights operated to and from London City Airport have complimentary catering. For more information visit ba.com/baconnect.

Payment Type: Visa Delta/Debit
Card Number: ************2062
Payment Total: GBP 249.80
Date / Issued by: 21 May 2006 /
British Airways, Newcastle, UK
IATA Number: 9URF8363
Endorsements: Pax nonref

Flight number: BA7947
From: Inverness
To: Gatwick (London) Terminal N
Depart: 17 Jul 2006 17:20
Arrive: 17 Jul 2006 19:10
Class: Domestic
Operated by: BA CONNECT
Booking status: Confirmed

Please note that all flights are designated non-smoking.

Ticket Number(s):
125-AAY1153969, 125-AAY1153970

Fare Details: GBP 162.00 + Tax/Fee/Charge GBP 87.80 = GBP 249.80
Fare breakdown: The price of your ticket includes a security and insurance surcharge and a fuel surcharge per sector levied by the carrier.
Please note that air travel is not subject to VAT therefore we do not issue VAT receipts.

BAGGAGE
Adult/child Baggage allowance is 1 piece per person
For detailed checked (hold) baggage allowance, including infant allowances, click the link below
http://ba.com/baggage

Baggage that exceeds allowances will incur a charge. No single item of baggage may weigh more than 32kg (70lbs).
For cabin bag allowance click the link below
http://ba.com/cabinbag

MANAGING OR MAKING CHANGES TO YOUR BOOKING
Click on the link below to access your booking:
http://ba.com/travel/managebooking/?eld=*******bookingRef=YG257YKG&lastname=BROWN

Please note that this link provides direct access to your booking. so please only forward this email if you want the recipient to access your booking and the related services.

Where applicable, if you wish to change the date or time of your flight, or cancel your booking, the cost of doing so will

8.2 Case study: Playmonday.com

Student book pages 322–329

Monday is a new, entirely web-based form of lottery. It was set up by Chariot.org.uk with the purpose of making it easier to win smaller amounts of money on a lottery, and also of giving more of the income directly to charities rather than to shareholders who have invested in the lottery company.

www.playmonday.com was launched on 20 April 2006 with a television advertising campaign. Monday, the Charities Lottery, unlike other lotteries, allows people playing the lottery to choose which charities the money goes to, from a list of charities given for that particular week. Charities are able to make people aware of what they do by explaining their purpose on the website.

By operating only online, Monday keeps its costs low, as no ticket is issued and no retailer or other person receives commission. Customers make their selection of numbers online by clicking on the numbers they want, and, as they do not have a paper ticket, they can never lose it! This means the chances of people not knowing they have won are gone.

As with any form of gambling, Monday does require people playing to be 18 or over.

1. What is different about Monday compared to other lotteries?
2. What are the advantages of running a lottery online?
3. Are there any possible disadvantages?

8.3 Plenary activity: Does it matter?

Student book pages 326–329

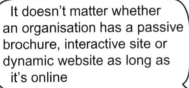

It doesn't matter whether an organisation has a passive brochure, interactive site or dynamic website as long as it's online

Discuss how much you agree with this view.

8.4 Introductory activity: Benefits to business

Student book pages 331–337

When a business operates online there are a number of key benefits that they can get compared to having only an offline presence. Using the questions below to help you, think about the benefits of trading online by answering each one carefully in relation to an online business that you know

1. When are they open?
2. Who can they sell to?
3. When do customers need to pay?
4. How can they tell what their competitors are doing?
5. How do they communicate with customers?
6. How do they monitor potential customers visiting their site?
7. What kinds of data do they hold (personal information, sales records, etc.) and why?
8. How do the business running costs compare with those of a retail store on the High Street?

8.5 Case study: Dixons and Currys and …

Student book pages 331–337

You may have noticed on the High Street that Dixons electrical stores have been converted into Currys Digital stores. (See Activity 7.2 in Unit 7.) This is because Dixons are going to move towards only online sales for smaller electrical items like MP3 player or iPods, whereas Currys will continue to sell larger items that customers may want to look at before buying them. The two brand names are both owned by the same company, so the company will benefit from reaching two different areas of the market – e-tailing and retailing.

1. Write down the names of at least three other retailers that you know of that have both retailing and e-tailing presences.
2. How do they cope with online and off-line customers?
3. Which services do they offer that are the same – are there any different ones?
4. How do they price their services on- and off-line?
5. Explain the benefits to those retailers of having an online rather than off-line presence.

Doing business online **185**

8.6 Discussion activity: Lowering costs

**Student book
pages 331–337**

Look at each of the areas of cost below and write how it would be lowered by operating only online, as opposed to off-line.

Cost	How online costs would be reduced relative to off-line
Staff	
Premises	
Electricity/gas	
Insurance	
Advertising	
Equipment	

1. Are there any costs that might go up as a result of trading only online?
2. What are these costs, and explain why they are likely to be higher than off-line.
3. Make recommendations for how they could be kept to a minimum.

8.7 Worksheet: Company websites

**Student book
pages 331–337**

See CD-ROM

Outcome 2

© Harcourt Education 2006

8.8 Discussion activity: Who benefits?

Student book pages 331–337

1. How does accessing online businesses help these customers?
2. How can a business benefit by attracting these customers?

A lady in a remote village with very poor bus services	
A person who needs wheelchair access when they are high street shopping	
A night-shift worker who needs to sleep all day	
A customer who is living abroad but wants to buy UK products	
A parent at home with a very young baby	
A person in who is housebound after major surgery and lives alone	

8.9 Research activity: Paying online

**Student book
pages 339–342, 346–348**

There are lots of different ways to pay online. Look up each of the methods below and give the advantages and disadvantages of using each for customers and for businesses.

Method	Advantages	Disadvantages
PayPal account		
Credit card		
Debit card		
Text message		

Which method would you recommend for a pizza business like Petra's Pizza (see Activities 8.16 and 8.17)?

8.10 Discussion activity: Fraud on the Internet

**Student book
pages 339–342**

There are seven main types of fraud that you may come across on the Internet. Fraud doesn't need to stop you buying goods or services online, but you should be careful who you give your details to, and watch out for common problems.

Problem 1: Rogue traders. These are people who take your details or your money and never actually supply the goods. They are no different in reality from rogue traders who operate face to face and who sell you something broken, dangerous or illegal: they are just using the web to do it.

Problem 2: Phishing. This is when you get emails from a source that pretends it is someone else; for example, an email that seems to be from your bank or a special offer from a car company. They are not really from who they say they are, and they want to steal your personal details.

8.10 Discussion activity: Fraud on the Internet (continued)

Problem 3: Identity fraud. Someone steals your identity or your credit card to buy things or use services in your name – you just get left with the bill. To avoid this you should be careful who you give your details to, and do not let your credit card out of your sight.

Problem 4: Lottery scams. You will be told you have won a prize (in a lottery that you never entered!) and need to ring an expensive telephone number or a pay a 'registration fee' to claim it. This means it will cost you money to find out you haven't won anything anyway.

Problem 5: Transferring money. You receive an email asking you to receive some money into a bank account on behalf of someone else. In return you will receive a percentage of the money. If you transferred the money you might be committing a criminal offence anyway. In the usual version of this fraud, the '419' or 'advance fee' fraud, you have to send some money first – if you do, you will lose that money, and possibly the entire contents of your bank account.

Problem 6: Chain emails. These emails ask you to pass them on to the next person. They are collecting details and web addresses so that they can compile lists and sell them for use in marketing or spamming – don't open them.

Problem 7: Share scams. These are the Internet version of the 'boiler room' scam, where offshore operations (beyond the reach of the EU's anti-spam laws) promote shares in non-existent companies, or shares that are overpriced and can't be traded.

For more information go to www.euroconsumer.org.uk, which gives further guidance on how to spot fraud attempts. Often the emails contain the message in the form of GIF images, so that anti-spam programs can't detect it.

Using the article above, ask other members of your class about their experience of any of these types of potential fraud. Put your results in the table below and see which are most common.

Problem	Number of people with experience of it
Problem 1: Rogue traders	
Problem 2: Phishing	
Problem 3: Identity fraud	
Problem 4: Lottery scams	
Problem 5: Transferring money	
Problem 6: Chain emails	
Problem 7: Share scams	

8.11 Worksheet: The most serious problem?

Student book pages 342–346

See CD-ROM

8.12 Research activity: Coping with unexpected demand

Student book pages 343–344, 346

One of the major issues that an online presence must take into account is that of being able to cope with the level of demand that the business will receive for its product or service. This means investing a lot of money into providing the best hardware, software and support to run the service. It is difficult to tell how much demand there will actually be, but too much demand can mean the website will be unable to cope, resulting in disappointed customers.

Research into the situations given below. What happened and what did this mean for the website and customers? Think of any other situations where a store coped well with high demand, or not so well.

The Inland Revenue launching their first site to help people pay their tax	
Amazon not being able to get products out to customers in time for Christmas in 2004	

8.13 Worksheet: Distribution

Student book pages 348–350

See CD-ROM

8.14 Plenary activity: Staffing

Student book pages 344–346

As people rely more and more on the use of websites, the number of staff and type of staff that are needed will change.

Banks

Banks used to employ staff to talk to customers face to face about loans, applications, mortgages and so on, as well as needing people to process cash, cheques and cards. Today many of a bank's staff work in call centres. Also many customers bank online, and they can obtain cash from 'through-the-wall' cash dispensers or via cashback at the supermarket checkout, so they never even go into their bank branch any more. Customers can apply for a loan and get the bank's agreement by email on the same day. This means that the customer is happy and the bank can provide a better service.

Supermarkets

The future of supermarkets is towards more online shopping, so customers do not visit the store. They are able to choose what they want from their own home. This saves them time and energy. Even in the shop, IT is changing the way people shop, as there are more self-service tills so that you buy your shopping yourself by swiping your own goods and credit card – you don't even get a sales assistant to help you with that!

1. Using these two examples to help you, what do you think will happen to the number of staff used in the following types of industry, based on the business trend towards making more use of online services?

    - leisure centres
    - cinemas
    - train travel
    - clothes shopping
    - beauty therapy
    - estate agencies.

2. What might be the feelings of staff working in those industries?

Doing business online

8.15 PowerPoint presentation: Online benefits

Student book pages 353–360

See CD-ROM

8.16 Worksheet: Petra's Pizza

Student book pages 356–360

See CD-ROM

8.17 Research activity: The pizza market

Student book pages 326–329, 356–358

To help Petra to understand what is happening in the pizza delivery market she has asked you to carry out research into local pizza companies to see what kind of websites they are offering, if any. Complete the following table with your results.

Business	Has no website	Passive website	Partially Interactive website	Interactive website

Discuss your findings with other students in your class and with your teacher.

Outcome 4

8.18 Worksheet: It's all in a name

Student book pages 331–332

See CD-ROM

8.19 Plenary activity: Should Petra go online?

Student book pages 353–360

You studied Petra's pizza delivery service and the pizza market in your local area for Activities 8.16 and 8.17. Using the information from these tasks, and making the most of the additional information you have collected in the other tasks in this unit, make recommendations for whether or not Petra should go online.

Reasons for going online – including why in this case ...	Reasons for not going online – including why in this case ...

Overall, what should she do?

Outcome 4

Unit 8 Exemplar assignment

Assignment 8.4

Background to the Assignment

For this assignment you are going to be advising a local pizza delivery business about the benefits of moving their business online.

Mr Cheesey's Pizzas are trading from a small High Street premises in Anytown. They have been trading for the past 10 years but Sally Nobile, who owns Cheesey's, is thinking that she should start to expand a bit by going online. Her sister has just come back from a holiday in America where she was able to order all of her meals online and have them delivered to the door. Sally is not completely convinced this is a good idea so has asked you to provide her with some information.

This assignment is aiming to help you achieve:

P5 Describe the benefits to a business organisation marketing a product or service online

M3 Explain the potential benefits for a business planning to go online.

Remember to include a bibliography at the end of your work with a list of all the websites you have used and clearly show information that you have collected from websites or text books with the author or site shown in brackets.

Task 1: Benefits of marketing a product or service online (P5)

Produce a leaflet giving Sally lots of advice about the benefits to a business of marketing a product or service online.

Task 2: Report (M3)

Write a report for Sally explaining the benefits if her business goes online. Make sure your comments relate to her pizza delivery business rather than general ones. You may use some of the topic headings below to help you and give her information about other pizza or food services that are already using online presences to benefit their businesses.

presence	marketing	response	financial
24-hour operation	access to different markets	delivery times	cash flow (money coming in and going out of the business)
equality	poor transport/ communication	out of hours business	debts
customer interest	transport	access	low cost
keeping up with competition		order tracking	cash handling
			ease of doing this

Student's work

Task 1

Going online?

There are lots of benefits for going on line now so it is something that all businesses should think about. This information leaflet will give you information about 6 good reasons to go online.

Benefit 1 A website is available 24 hours a day. It never shuts. This is a really good reason to go online because your business can be available even when you are not.

Benefit 2 It doesn't matter whether your business is small or large. All business can compete in the same way online if they get people to know their site and look after it.

Benefit 3 Customers logging on to a website are likely to be interested straight away so unlike a shop where you would need to go off and buy the product or service on the website they could buy it straight away.

Benefit 4 It can be possible to get new customers to use your business because people who have difficulties getting out of their homes or work long hours can still access your service

Benefit 5 Order tracking can be done easily online for example parcel delivery services can tell their customers exactly when a parcel was delivered using online tracking.

Benefit 6 Customers usually need to pay first when they are buying goods online. This is good for businesses because it means they don't have to wait ages for their money

By Charlotte Brown BTEC First Business Unit 8

Charlotte Brown BTEC First Business Unit 8

Assignment 8.4

Task 2

Report for Mr Cheesey's Pizza Business

Mr Cheesey's should go online because it would mean that they could get more customers. This is because customers who cannot get to the shop could order over the internet. This would mean they could get higher sales and make more profits. Sally could be open 24 hours a day because that would mean that she could get customers who are coming home late or early in the morning. This would be good for her business as she could get more orders. As she is a small business owner Sally could compete with other business like Pizza Hut or Pizza Express by being online and having her own website because she could take money from customers straight away when they order. This would mean she wouldn't need to wait until they delivered the pizza to the door and her driver would not need to carry cash around with her as much. Because the orders could go straight in to the shop she would be able to start cooking the order straight away if she had fast internet access and this would mean that there might be less mistakes because of people not hearing properly on the telephone. This would save her money if all of her orders were right the first time. It would also stop people phoning up when they shouldn't to order pizzas for other people. They would have to pay for them first. By being online she is able to actually see how much her competitors are charging and make really quick changes to her prices or put special offers for web customers eg 10% off with a code to be used online.

Assessor feedback

Task 1

You have produced a really attractive leaflet giving clear reasons why Sally should think about going online. Well done.

Task 2

You have made a good start on your report but remember for Merit Level you need to use the right report format – you should have an introduction with a background to why you need to do the report and then any information you want to add needs to be put under different headings. You have included lots of good ideas but they need to be organised even more clearly. Make sure you link them together under different headings.

You could also think of adding examples of what other businesses are doing for food delivery including a list of websites that you have used to get your information to help you.

Finally you should also add a conclusion giving a summary of what you have found out to end your report. You have made a good start towards M3 so please improve it to get full achievement of this criterion.

Unit 8 Resources

Additional resources that can be used to support student learning of this Unit are:

Textbooks

Carysforth, C. and Neild, M., *BTEC First Business* (Heinemann, 2006)

Anderton, A., *GCSE Business Studies* (Causeway Press, 1998)

Cumming, T., *Little E, Big Business, How to Make a Profit Online* (Virgin Books, 2001)

Dransfield, R. *et al.*, *BTEC National Business: Student Book* (Heinemann, 2004). This resource may be useful for those students operating at Distinction level who require additional information to help them.

Fardon, M., Nuttall, C. and Prokopiw, J., *GCSE Applied Business* (Osborne Books, 2002)

Holden, G., *Starting an Online Business for Dummies* (Hungry Minds, 2002)

Wall, J. and Wales, N., *Nuffield–BP Business and Economics for GCSE* (2nd edn, Collins, 2001)

Websites

There are lots of websites available to help in the preparation for work area. Some useful sites that may provide additional information and ideas include:

www.bized.ac.uk	Bized business education site
www.euroconsumer.org.uk	Euroconsumer advice site with online information
www.startups.co.uk	Business Start Up site with links to online business
www.crimereduction.gov.uk/etailing	Government site set up with tips to avoid fraud
www.smallbusiness.co.uk	Small business site with links to online trading
www.bytestart.co.uk	Small online business support
www.electronic-payments.co.uk	Government site giving neutral advice on online payment methods for businesses. (In a fast-changing market, its database should not be assumed to be up to date.)

Unit 9 Exploring business enterprise

Unit overview

Unit 9 is a specialist unit for the BTEC First Certificate and BTEC First Diploma qualifications in Business. It *cannot* be completed in conjunction with Unit 10. The unit aims to help students understand the range and complexity of issues involved in preparing for business enterprise, and some of the key elements of running a business.

The unit seeks to prepare students for business enterprise by considering all aspects of business planning and self-employment. The unit starts by asking students to consider the issues surrounding self-employment by focusing on their own individual strengths and weaknesses. These are then developed into possible business ideas that include the benefits of running your own business.

The unit emphasises the importance of business planning by looking at all of the areas of a business plan individually and asking students to conduct research into the legal, financial and marketing aspects of business preparation. Learners are also encouraged to consider different sources of help when planning to run a business, including their own financial situation and that of friends, colleagues and relatives that may be able to help them. They are also encouraged to consider the support of organisations such as banks, business advisors or the Prince's Trust.

By producing a suitable business plan, students are able to work towards achievement of the higher levels of this unit by justifying their choices and making judgements and recommendations about the viability of the business enterprise they are planning for.

Suggested activities

The table on the following pages shows how activities in this Assessment and Delivery Resource cover the four different outcomes of the Unit. There are a variety of tasks including discussion material, worksheets, case studies and presentation material.

The research tasks have been prepared to allow students to gather evidence in note form to help them produce their own work.

How this unit will be assessed

To gain a Pass, learners will need to:

P1 describe how knowledge of personal strengths and weaknesses can be applied to preparing for and contributing to a business

P2 describe how regulations and laws for small businesses can affect preparation for business

P3 describe how small businesses prepare to market and sell products or services

P4 describe the financial issues that can affect preparation for business

P5 outline the contents of a business plan when starting and running a business

P6 describe the sources of advice and support available when preparing for business.

To gain a Merit requires learners to complete all the Pass requirements plus the Merit requirements, where they need to:

M1 explain, using examples, the benefits of running a business

M2 analyse the different aspects that will affect preparation for business

M3 explain the components of a business plan and the reasons for preparing one.

To gain a Distinction requires a learner to complete all the Pass and Merit requirements plus the Distinction requirement, where they need to:

D1 evaluate the issues that need to be considered when starting and running a business

D2 make and justify recommendations for starting a business.

Learning outcomes

The unit is based on the following learning outcomes:

1 Understand how to prepare for business

2 Know how different aspects affect preparation for business

3 Understand how to start and run a business.

© Harcourt Education 2006

At-a-glance activities

Activity type and description	Delivery notes	Extra resources	Links to grading criteria	Links to textbook
Outcome 1 Understand how to prepare for business				
9.1 Introductory worksheet: SWOT	This activity asks students to focus on what they are good at and not so good at, and consider how these things can affect their ability to run their own business.	Worksheet on CD-ROM	P1	Pages 364–366
9.2 Worksheet: What is most important to me?	This activity asks students to think about what is important to them as part of considering their own strengths and weaknesses, and whether or not setting up a business would be suitable for them. By analysing each of the different issues or benefits they can also work on M2 and possibly also D1.	Worksheet on CD-ROM.	P1, M2, D1	Pages 364–370
9.3 Case study: Looking for a bar in the market?	Stoats Porridge Bars was launched in 2005 by a young entrepreneur. The study shows how spotting a trend or gap can help an entrepreneur to be successful.		P1, M2	Pages 368–370
9.4 Research activity: Sources of finance	This activity asks students to consider where they could get investment money from or how they could be supported during the time when a business is being set up.	Leaflets from banks, trusts, Enterprise Centres, etc.	P1, M2	Pages 366–368
Outcome 2 Know how different aspects affect preparation for business				
9.5 Worksheet: *Business Pages*	This newspaper article activity asks students to give an outline of the three main types of business ownership studied in this unit, and the advantages and disadvantages of each for the type of business that they are planning to set up.	Worksheet on CD-ROM	P2, M2	Pages 373–375

Activity type and description	Delivery notes	Extra resources	Links to grading criteria	Links to textbook
9.6 Plenary activity: True or false?	These statements relate to the legal aspects of setting up a business with true or false answers for students to tick. An extension to the activity would be for students to explain the importance of each element, e.g. insurance, certificates and so on.	Pen	P2	Pages 373–379
9.7 Worksheet: Reaching customers	Students are asked to consider the different ways that businesses can reach their customers, and give examples for each. There is also space for the student to enter the same information for the business they plan to set up as part of this unit.	Worksheet on CD-ROM	P3	Pages 379–386
9.8 Worksheet: Local or national?	Within this activity, students consider different methods of promotion in relation to a restaurant business, and whether local or national advertising is suitable. They are then asked to apply some of the ideas to their own business idea.	Worksheet on CD-ROM	P3, M2	Pages 379–386
9.9 Worksheet: Start-up or operating costs?	This activity asks students to work out whether costs are start-up or operating costs. They are then asked to consider how these costs relate to their own business.	Worksheet on CD-ROM	P4, M2	Pages 386–390
9.10 Discussion activity: Are finances important?	This discussion asks students to consider how important finances actually are – are they the most important factor, and do they make a large number of businesses fail? This activity could be extended by also looking at profits vs cash flow, or the importance of customer service.		P4, M2, D1	Pages 386–390
9.11 Case study: Questioning questionnaires	Students are asked to consider what is wrong with the questionnaire researching the demand for onion and banana pasties. They are then asked to make their own questionnaire to be used for their business idea.	Access to PC or materials for producing questionnaires	P3, M2	Pages 379–386
9.12 Discussion activity: Promotion by email	This background material to the use of email for promotion gives students an idea of some of the associated difficulties, including legislation preventing the use of spam.		P3, M2	Pages 379–386

Activity type and description	Delivery notes	Extra resources	Links to grading criteria	Links to textbook
9.13 Plenary activity: Cash-flow forecasting	This activity gives students a cash-flow forecast to look at and then consider what advice they would give. As in many new businesses, cash-flow is negative at the start of the business, and advice for the new business owner could be on getting a larger loan (which should be satisfactory as long as it is only for a short time), or on ways of reducing costs or increasing receipts, etc., or spreading out purchases more evenly.		P4, M2	Pages 386–390
Outcome 3 Understand how to start and run a business				
9.14 Introductory activity: What is in a business plan?	This activity asks students to think about what should be in a business plan. This task may be used as revision just before the business plan task after the use of the PowerPoint presentation available on CD, or as an introductory activity.		P5	Pages 394–395
9.15 Worksheet: Can you control it?	This activity considers those elements that a business can control and those that are outside its control but could be planned for (contingency planning). At Distinction level, students can be encouraged to consider how a well-planned business should be able to prepare for most eventualities, whether inside or outside their control.	Worksheet on CD-ROM	P5, M3, D1, D2	Pages 396–399
9.16 Worksheet: The business plan	This simple business plan template can be used by students to fill in their data. Students should also be encouraged to add additional information such as spreadsheets to the plan. To work towards the Merit and Distinction criteria, they are also asked to give a judgement about the plan.	Worksheet on CD-ROM	P5, M3, D2	Pages 394–401
9.17 Discussion activity: Advice and support	Students are encouraged to consider the different sources of advice or information available. They will explore what those agencies do and how they could help with their individual business, then discuss with other students.	Leaflets from websites for these organisations	P6, M2	Pages 400–401

Activity type and description	Delivery notes	Extra resources	Links to grading criteria	Links to textbook
9.18 Presentation activity: You as the business advisor	This activity asks students to consider their top tips and recommendations for others producing a business plan. What are the limitations/benefits?		P5, M3	Pages 400–401
9.19 PowerPoint presentation: Elements of a business plan	This presentation gives some useful tips and pointers for students on elements of the business plan and how to complete it.	Projector	P1, M1, D1	Pages 394–401

Unit 9 Activities

9.1 Worksheet: SWOT

Student book
pages 364–366

See CD-ROM

9.2 Worksheet: What is most important to me?

Student book
pages 364–370

See CD-ROM

9.3 Case study: Looking for a bar in the market?

Student book
pages 368–370

Tony Stone won Lothian and Borders Shell Livewire Young Entrepreneur of the Year 2006 by producing a new type of porridge-based healthy alternative to the sugary or unhealthy goods that he was eating for breakfast.

He launched Stoats Porridge Bars as he had also noticed that sales of porridge oats had gone up 25 per cent in 2004. These bars are like an alternative to a Burger Bar by offering different types of porridge in convenient tubs!

He and his business partner Bob Arnott now serve around 400 tubs of porridge per week and travel throughout the country. They opened their first permanent porridge bar in June 2006.

1. What was the original idea behind Stoats Porridge Bars?
2. What information do you think helped Tony to think of his final idea?
3. What do you think Stoats Porridge Bars have been successful?

© Harcourt Education 2006

Outcome 1

9.4 Research activity: Sources of finance

Student book pages 366–368

Carry out research into where you could get sources of finance to help set up your business. This may be in the form of money to invest, or even support from your family or friends in giving you somewhere to live or resources to use during the time when a business is not yet making money. Answer yes or no for each type of potential investor, giving examples where possible.

Investor	Could they give me a one-off contribution of money, equipment resources, etc.?	Could they support me with expenses or money while I establish the business?
Myself		
My family		
My friends		
People I work with		
Banks and building societies		
Young Enterprise Funds		
Prince's Trust		
Neighbours		
Business grants from the EU		
Job centre		

Outcome 1

9.5 Worksheet: *Business Pages*

Student book
pages 373–375

See CD-ROM

9.6 Plenary activity: True or false?

Student book
pages 373–379

Mark the following statements as true or false.

Item	True	False
A tax return must be kept for up to five years		
All businesses need to have a fire certificate		
If a business employs five or more people, it must carry out a formal risk assessment		
Leasing is when a business hires equipment by paying for it each month		
Many forms, e.g. tax returns or accident reports, can be sent online		
PAYE stands for Pay After You have Earned		
The current standard rate of VAT is 17.5%		
The insurance available at work to protect against claims for injuries or accidents is called Employee's Liability Insurance		
VAT is a tax that is paid on many but not all transactions		

9.7 Worksheet: Reaching customers

Student book pages 379–386

See CD-ROM

9.8 Worksheet: Local or national?

Student book pages 379–386

See CD-ROM

9.9 Worksheet: Start-up or operating costs?

Student book pages 386–390

See CD-ROM

9.10 Discussion activity: Are finances important?

Student book pages 386–390

Discuss the following:

1. How important are finances for a business?
2. What makes many businesses go out of business?
3. How important is finance to your business idea?

9.11 Case study: Questioning questionnaires

Student book pages 379–386

Look at the questionnaire below.

1. Write what is wrong with it – how could these things be put right?
2. Is there anything good about it?

Onion and Banana Pasties

What is your name?
How old are you?   16–17   17–18   18–24   25–36
How often do you eat pasties? Every day   A couple of times a week   Occasionally   Sometimes   Never
Where do you live?
How much would you pay for a pasty?   50p   60p   80p   90p   100p   120p
Where do you buy pasties from?
Which is your favourite flavour of pasty?
Would you eat an onion and banana pasty?
Which of the following is most likely to persuade you to buy a onion and banana pasty? Please tick Sales coupon TV advert Internet pop-up Free trial
What gender are you? Please circle Male or Female
How many times a week do you watch or read the following Radio   _____ per week Television   _____ per week Newspapers   _____ per week Internet   _____ per week Email   _____ per week

3. Now write a questionnaire that you can use for your business planning idea, making sure you avoid the mistakes that are given here.

9.12 Discussion activity: Promotion by email

Student book pages 379–386

Email is also useful a useful way to let customers know about your business. Photographs of hotels and swimming pools can be used to promote a service offered by a holiday business. Video clips or sound files could also be added so that the target audience can get a realistic idea about the product or service on offer.

Email can also be used to give incentives to customers within a relatively short time: for example, if they respond to the email within 48 hours, they can benefit from a discount. Another possibility is to print out a voucher with a unique number, e.g. a discount voucher for money off in a supermarket. It is quick and easy to send an email message to a large number of customers, and the business can monitor how good the email is by watching if people go straight to the site.

However, unsolicited email (spam) is now illegal under the The Privacy and Electronic Communications Regulations 2003 (which implement an EC Directive), so the business must first know who they are sending the emails to, and ensure that the recipients have agreed to accept messages. Some customers may find email annoying and get the wrong impression of the company – they may just delete it and not read it.

It is interesting, however, that according to the Information Commissioner, who enforces The Privacy and Electronic Communications Regulations, only 2 per cent of junk email is sent by rogue companies based in the UK. The other 98 per cent is sent by businesses (mostly US) that are not governed by UK law!

1. Based on the article above, write in the boxes below what you think are the advantages and disadvantages of using email for promotions.
2. Can you think of any others?
3. How might these advantages and disadvantages affect the way that a business prepares to send out emails about its products or services?

Advantages	Disadvantages

9.13 Plenary activity: Cash-flow forecasting

Student book pages 386–390

Look at the cash flow forecast given below.

	Jan	Feb	Mar	Apr
	£	£	£	£
Opening bank balance	5000	(2100)	(200)	(2300)
Receipts				
Cash sales	2000	3000	4000	4000
Credit sales	0	1000	1000	2000
Total receipts	2000	4000	5000	6000
Payments				
Purchases of stock	4000	0	5000	0
Wages	2000	2000	2000	2000
Telephone bills	100	100	100	100
Shop and fixtures	3000	0	0	0
Total payments	9100	2100	7100	2100
Closing bank balance	(2100)	(200)	(2300)	1600

1. What do you notice about it?
2. Which recommendations would you make to the manager of this business?
3. How important is the preparation of a good cash-flow forecast for a business?
4. Produce a cash-flow forecast for your business idea.

9.14 Introductory activity: What is in a business plan?

Student book pages 394–395

Write or draw the items that you think should be contained within a business plan on the diagram below. Explain each item and why it is important to prepare a business plan containing all the necessary information.

9.15 Worksheet: Can you control it?

Student book pages 396–399

See CD-ROM

Outcome 3

9.16 Worksheet: The business plan

Student book pages 394–401

See CD-ROM

9.17 Discussion activity: Advice and support

Student book pages 400–401

Complete the table below by considering how each of the agencies given below can provide help and guidance to new businesses. Discuss how they could help you with your new business.

Source	What do they do?	How can they help you with your business?
Business Link		
Banks		
Chamber of Commerce		
Local authority		
Solicitors		
Accountants		
Prince's Trust		

Outcome 3

Exploring business enterprise | 211

9.18 Presentation activity: You as the business advisor!

Student book pages 400–401

Now that you have researched and produced your own business and business plan, produce a poster giving a set of recommendations about how and why a business plan should be written, including a set of tips for the best way to complete this process. Mention its limitations too.

9.19 PowerPoint presentation: Elements of a business plan

Student book pages 394–401

See CD-ROM

Outcome 3 © Harcourt Education 2006

Unit 9 Exemplar assignment

Assignment 9.1: It's all about me!

Background to the assignment

This assignment is aiming to help you achieve:

P1 Describe how knowledge of personal strengths and weaknesses can be applied to preparing for an contributing to a business

Task 1 (P1)

Complete the self-assessment sheets 1 and 2 to help you work out your own personal strengths and weaknesses.

Task 2 (P1)

Looking at your personal strengths:

How could these help you to prepare for and contribute to running your own business?

How would they help you to run a business?

Task 3 (P1)

Now look at your personal weaknesses:

How might these affect the way that you would run a business?

What could you do to try to make sure they would not affect your running of a business?

Self-assessment task 1

Complete this self-assessment by ticking for each area whether or not you think it is a strength or weakness for you personally and by describing why you think this.

Area	S	W	Description
Business qualifications			
Knowledge of business from family of friends			
Work experience			
IT skills			
Understanding of accounts			
Understanding of law			
Filling out paperwork			
Persuading customers to buy from you			
Thinking of new ways of doing things or changing ideas			
Thinking of reasons why something isn't working			
Able to talk confidently to a variety of different people to help the business (networking)			

Exemplar assignment

Self-assessment task 2

This task is trying to work out the kind of contribution that you would be able to make to a business by considering how much of your time you could contribute, how organised you would be with that time and so on.

Statement	Very like me	A bit like me	Not like me	Very unlike me
I am good at working out which are important tasks that I must do first				
I write lists to help me be organised				
I am willing to listen to advice so that I can improve				
I use a diary to help me organise what I need to do				
I always wear a watch and arrive on time				
I don't get easily stressed, I enjoy challenges				
I am able to get access to money that I could invest in a business				
I have family or friends who could lend me money to start a business				
I have lots of free time that I could use to start up a business				
I give myself a treat if I feel I have done something well				
I am a reliable person and always get the job done				
I have got spare space at home where I could set up an office or space for my business				
I am happy to give up my time with my friends and family to work long hours				
I like to find problems and sort them out				
I work well with lots of different groups of people				

Exploring business enterprise

Student's work

Task 1

Area	S	W	Description
Business qualifications	✗		I am doing BTEC First Business this year and I hope to get a Merit. I am also redoing my Maths GCSE so that will help me to be better at business.
Knowledge of business from family of friends		✗	Nobody in my family has run their own business so I don't really know what that is like. My brother works in the local shop so I have talked to him a bit about what he does but I am not very sure about it.
Work experience		✗	I am looking for a part-time job but I don't have one yet.
IT skills	✗		I have got IT skills from GCSE at school and I know how to use all the main packages.
Understanding of finance	✗		I know a little bit about finance from doing Unit 3 of the BTEC First but not a lot.
Understanding of law		✗	I don't know much about the law side of business so I would need to look this up.
Filling out paperwork	✗		I have got neat handwriting and I think I can understanding most paperwork.
Persuading customers to buy from you	✗		I like talking to people so think I would be able to persuade people to buy things from me.
Thinking of new ways of doing things or changing ideas		✗	I don't really like looking for new ways of doing things I just like to get on with what I am doing.
Thinking of reasons why something isn't working		✗	I like to get help from other people if something is not working, I am not very good at finding it out myself.
Able to talk confidently to a variety of different people to help the business (networking)		✗	I am not very confident at talking with other business people because I think I might say something wrong.

Exemplar assignment © Harcourt Education 2006

Task 2

Statement	Very like me	A bit like me	Not like me	Very unlike me
I am good at working out which are important tasks that I must do first		✗		
I write lists to help me be organised			✗	
I am willing to listen to advice so that I can improve		✗		
I use a diary to help me organise what I need to do			✗	
I always wear a watch and arrive on time.	✗			
I don't get easily stressed, I enjoy challenges	✗			
I am able to get access to money that I could invest in a business				✗
I have family or friends who could lend me money to start a business				✗
I have lots of free time that I could use to start up a business.			✗	
I give myself a treat if I feel I have done something well	✗			
I am a reliable person and always get the job done		✗		
I have got spare space at home where I could set up an office or space for my business				✗
I am happy to give up my time with my friends and family to work long hours		✗		
I like to find problems and sort them out			✗	
I work well with lots of different groups of people		✗		

Task 3

Task 3

From doing the two self-assessments I can see that I have got some strengths and some weaknesses to prepare for and contribute to a business.

Strengths

I have got skills in business, IT and finance. These are important skills that I will need for my business to help me know how the business is going to run and to be able to get money and produce statements for other people to look at.

I am also good at filling out paperwork which will be really important for my business because there is always a lot of paperwork to do or if I need to do it online I can use my IT skills to help me. I am also good at dealing with customers so this should help me to get customers to spend their money with me.

Task 3

I like listening to the advice of other people so this would help me to listen and get told things to help me improve my business.

I don't get easily stressed so this is a good thing for me going in to business. Running a business can be stressful but I should be ok with this. I also am good at giving myself a treat like a day off if something has gone well but I must make sure I don't do it too much or my business might go wrong.

I think I would be ok with giving up some time with my friends and family to work on my business especially if it is something I really like.

Weaknesses

I have got some weaknesses. The first one is that I don't have much experience of business in a real life situation because my family don't own a business and I have not got a part-time job. I am looking for one so this should get better and my brother does tell me little bits about his job. I need to find out more if I am going to run a good business.

I don't know anything about law so I would need to find out lots of information before I could run my business. I also would feel shy talking to people about my business if they are very experienced like other business people. I need to overcome this because they could really help me as I find it difficult to sort out problems myself.

I will need to think about how organised I am because I don't usually wear a watch or get to places on time. I also don't like keeping a diary. I may have to change my mind about this because if I am late it might annoy my customers and if I am not organised they may not come back to me again.

At home I have not got anyone who can lend me any money to start up a business and I don't have any money of my own so I will need to borrow the money from someone like a bank. There is no spare room where I live to run a business so I would need to run it from somewhere else which will cost more.

Assessor feedback

You have completed this task really well Jemma, well done. You have thought very carefully about the different strengths and weaknesses that you have and how you can relate them to starting up your own new business.

By thinking about the things that you realise you are good at and the things that you need to work on you can help yourself to produce really good work for this unit. You realise that law might be difficult for you so you will need to work carefully on this area within the assignment. You will learn lots about law and make sure you check that you understand it as we go along.

P1 certainly achieved!

Exemplar assignment

Unit 9 Resources

Additional resources that can be used to support student learning of this Unit are:

Textbooks

Carysforth, C. and Neild, M., *BTEC First Business* (Heinemann, 2006)

Barrow, C. and Barrow, P., *The Business Plan Workbook* (3rd edn, Kogan Page, 1998)

Golzen, G., *Working for Yourself* (18th edn, Kogan Page, 1998)

Vass, J., *The Which? Guide to Starting Your Own Business* (Which? Books, 1999)

Williams, S., *Lloyds TSB Small Business Guide* (13th edn, Penguin Books, 2000)

Wisdom, J., *Checklists and Operating Forms for Small Businesses* (Wiley, 1997)

Dransfield, R. *et al.*, *BTEC National Business: Student Book* (Heinemann, 2004). This resource may be useful for those students operating at Distinction level who require additional information to help them.

Websites

There are lots of websites available to help in the preparation for work area. Some useful sites that may provide additional information and ideas include:

www.bized.ac.uk	Bized business education site
www.businesslink.gov.uk	Support on all aspects of business including training and development
www.biz-in-a-box.co.uk	One of several companies that provide help in registering companies
www.bplans.org.uk	Business planning site
www.businesslink.gov.uk	Government-supported business planning site
www.businessplanhelp.co.uk	Tips and ideas for business planning
www.chamberonline.co.uk	Chambers of Commerce Online
www.dti.gov.uk	Department of Trade and Industry
www.ico.gov.uk	Information Commissioner's Office: provides guidance on the Data Protection Act, the Freedom of Information Act, and the Privacy and Electronic Communications Regulations
www.shell-livewire.org	New business start-up site aimed at 16–30-year-olds
www.smallbusinessadvice.org.uk	Small Business Advice Service
www.princes-trust.org.uk	Prince's Trust website